THIS, THAT, AND THE OTHER THING

This, That,
and
The Other Thing

by
Reginald T. Townsend

Illustrations by
F. G. COOPER

Essay Index Reprint Series

BOOKS FOR LIBRARIES PRESS
FREEPORT, NEW YORK

STANDARD BOOK NUMBER:
8369-1112-1

LIBRARY OF CONGRESS CATALOG CARD NUMBER:
75-84344

PRINTED IN THE UNITED STATES OF AMERICA

Foreword

NOT long since we were having a friendly argument with a friend about the value of memories. Now, our friend, while really an amiable and delightful chap, is inclined to a certain cynicism and a rather morbid view of life. He claimed that mankind would be better off if it had been denied the privilege of being able to look back into the past the way it has been denied the privilege of peering into the future. "Memories," he argued, "are at best bitter. For even the pleasant ones have a feeling of regret. If they were pleasant we want to live them over again and we can't; hence they become bitter."

While there is undoubtedly much truth in this, we cannot subscribe to it wholeheartedly. Many of the pleasantest occurrences of our life have been so spontaneous that they could not possibly be repeated, and we should hesitate, even fear, to try to live them over again. Yet some of these are the pleasantest of memories, and we derive the utmost pleasure in recalling them. And there is no trace of bitterness in our recollection. So our dour friend must be wrong in his generalization.

Many of the essays that compose this little volume are memories. We would jot them down from time to time—little anecdotes that amused us—putting them down would recall others, and we derived no little amusement and pleasure from them. After some hesitation we published them in *Country Life*. To our intense astonishment they seemed to be favourably received. People wrote and asked about them. They even suggested our putting them into book form. This struck a sympathetic chord, for one of our secret ambitions—like a million other people, we imagine—is to write a book. We have even started two or three novels, but something went wrong each time. We had good ideas, good plots, but somehow we could never make them jell, as it were. Probably the truth is that we are not at all equipped to write novels. Anyway, by publishing our little essays in book form we can at least say that we have published a book. So, in fear and trembling, we have assembled our pen children under one heading and we herewith deliver them into your tender hands. Be not too severe with them, and remember, whatever else they may lack, they are at least sincere; and that, no matter what the outcome may be, we have enjoyed writing them and have enjoyed, still more, seeing them in print.

REGINALD T. TOWNSEND.

"Treeptops,"
Oyster Bay, L. I.
1928.

CONTENTS

TO

A. F. G.

In Praise of Dawns

OF ALL the hours of day dawn we suppose is the most unpopular. To most people the mere mention of the word is provocative of a shudder. "The cold gray dawn" is what it is and always will be no doubt for most of us. Yet this is scarcely just, for there is nothing lovelier than the dawn of a fine summer's day—save possibly a golden sunset. Apparently it takes a poet to appreciate a dawn, for they have rhapsodized over "rosy-fingered dawn" since time immemorial. Yet we have an appreciation for dawns, and we are not a poet. Far from it. We couldn't scan a line of verse though our life depended on it, and we shouldn't recognize a pentameter if we met one.

Just how we acquired an affection for the dawn or how we ever got out of bed early enough to see one is lost in the mists of time, but we've seen many since the initial dawn, and

under many circumstances—pleasant and otherwise. If we recall correctly, our first dawn was
"when we were very young"—about Christopher
Robin's age, we should judge. The Angel of
Death hovered about our little household, and
we were awakened by the commotion that this
dread presence always brings. Sleep was out of
the question, so we took up a position at the
nursery window. Even to-day, after a score and
more years, we can still see the scene as we kept
watch at the window. How softly and beautifully
the dawn came up over the sleeping city—the
faint noises, the slowly dimming lights, and the
first rosy flush that heralded the coming day. We
were too young then to grasp the full significance
of death, but we felt a calm presence about us,
and the hour wove a spell of comfort and peace
over hearts sorely tried.

However, there have been many more dawns
witnessed under more lively circumstances than
this one, we must admit. One in particular we
recall when at a college prom we danced the
whole night through. How delicious it was with
nerves atingle to leave the feverish glamour of
the dancing floor and the strident beat of the
orchestra and to stroll out into the cool of the
early morning. How restful to sit upon the

parapet of the old college building and watch
the stars grow dim one by one and the gay Japanese lanterns grow pallid while that eerie light
which presages another day spread its wings over
the landscape at our feet. All the while there came
to our ears, borne faintly upon the fresh spring
breeze, the soft strains of music, made glamorous
by distance.

And we love to think of those strident dawns
when on a rash venture the more daring of us
dashed for the beach and dove into the surf for
that most exhilarating of plunges, a dip in the
sea at dawn. Or of that dawn when, returning
from a fancy dress ball, clad in silken breeches
and peruke, we encountered the milkman, who
greeted us impudently with "Hey, George Washington, go to bed." Even that dawn on the Rigi
whose spell was broken for us by the efforts of
the tourist lady to rouse her corpulent spouse
from the depths of slumber into which he per-
sisted in falling while the sun rose, a golden ball,
still brings a smile.

Somehow, in travelling one seems to come in
contact with the dawn more often than not.
Perhaps it is because one does not sleep soundly
on the train, or the unusual noises of a boat make
one restive. We can remember one ghastly night

spent on a lonely pier waiting for a small lake steamer that was due at 11 P. M. Hour after hour we sat perched on a spike trying to pierce the darkness, not daring to go to a hotel for fear we should miss the boat, and getting more and more drugged with lack of sleep as the hours wore on. Eventually, at 8 A. M., in full daylight, the boat appeared and we dragged ourself, more dead than alive, up the gangway.

And there was a dawn we particularly remember when we were going on leave in war time. The compartment was crowded with French civilians and American soldiers in about equal numbers. Most of the night was passed in a titanic effort to open the window on the part of the Americans and an equally fierce struggle to close it on the part of the French. However, as the compartment was crowded with soldiers the Yanks won the day. At Rouen a British staff officer, resplendent with gold lace and red trimmings, got into the car. Glancing around rather haughtily and finding no seat, and no one apparently going to offer him one, he took up a position near the door. Stiffly he stood, straight as a poker. An hour passed; we awoke from a doze to find him still standing, erect but sagging a bit. Through the long hours of the night he stood it out, but when dawn came at last it found him, gold lace and fancy trimmings and all, stretched out at full length on the floor, surrounded by the muddy boots of Yank soldiers and French civilians. That dawn, you will agree, saw a strange sight indeed.

But there came a time when we were to become an intimate companion of the dawn, a time when we were to look and watch and wait for Aurora as one awaits the coming of a lover. We had taken up the serious business of life in a mill on the Saguenay River, a great mill whose wheels turned busily both night and day. It was our duty to watch certain of those wheels throughout the long hours of the night. The room we worked in was full of steam and strident with harsh noises. Stripped to the waist we took up our position by the machines at dusk and prepared to watch the slow pageant of the night unroll before our eyes. About three or three-thirty in the morning, weary in flesh and in spirit from our never-ending battle with the demons of sleep, who sought by might and main to close our leaden eyelids, we would wander to the open doorway of the mill to get a whiff of pine-laden air and to gaze across the woods and streams wrapped in silence about us. As we looked across the valley where the lordly Saguenay pursued its roily course, we would catch a glimpse of the faintest tinge of pink on the snow that crowned the summits of the surrounding Laurentians. As we watched, the pink turned to rose, the rose to flame, and in an instant the mighty range was afire with a golden blaze that leaped and danced along its peaks like a thing alive. From two to five minutes the gorgeous spectacle endured, and then the day was upon us. Hope sprang eternal once more. The long night was done; rest and peace awaited us.

Do you wonder then that though we witnessed this spectacle hundreds of times we never failed to thrill to it? And do you wonder that we have a strange kinship with the dawn? And finally, do you wonder that to-day we still love to have the light of early dawn come stealing softly through the open window and, touching our eyelids, awaken us gently? What could be finer than to lie in a state of blissful semiconsciousness and hear the chorus of the birds swelling from a few faint notes to a final crescendo of liquid music, while overhead the sky reflects the softest pastel shades imaginable?

Yes, we can truthfully say, the dawn does mean something to us, and a something rather more, thank God, than just the cold, bleak harbinger of yet another day.

The Lure of the Auction

EVER since we can remember, auctions
have held a strange fascination for us.
The little red flag with "Auction To-
day" inscribed on it holds the same lure for us
that a piece of red flannel is said to hold for a
bullfrog.

A decade or so ago those gay little banners
were more common than they are to-day, and
one could find them by the score on the principal
streets of our big cities. Generally the type of
goods to be auctioned were cast-offs from the
pre-Victorian era—what-nots, Rogers groups,
new art lamps, easels, and all manner of furnish-
ings considered *chic* in that misguided day.

To-day the auction rooms—like the goods for
disposal in them—have taken on the air of impressive and dignified salons, not to be approached
lightly nor without a fairly well-filled purse. But
though they may change the surroundings, im-

prove the goods to be sold, even make auction-
eering one of the fine arts, none the less the
auction will always have a strong hold on even
the humblest of us—that is, while human nature
remains what it is. For an auction is a gamble
just as much as Wall Street or poker, and who
knows but that at any moment one may make
a lucky find for a mere pittance. It is, in short,
the old bait of something for nothing—as fascinating and as will-o'-the-wispish as ever it was.

Personally, though we've followed auctions
hither and yon, up and down these last twenty
years, we've never made a really priceless find,
but at the same time we've never been badly
cheated. Indeed, the auctioneer's cry of "Going,
going, gone" is still sweet music in our ears.

When we were still a schoolboy—thousands
of years ago—it used to be a favourite diversion
on our way home from school to drop in at the
various auction rooms that lay in our homeward
path. Many a glorious afternoon we had shouting out bids gleefully, until one fine day, misjudg-
ing our competitors' bidding ability or maybe
having grown too venturesome, we found ourselves the prospective owner of a pair of Ming
(so-called—Woolworth probably) vases at a
figure which, while not much in actual money,

was certainly a lot more than the vases were worth and, even more important, a great deal more than the sum total of our entire wealth.

Best draw a veil over the scene as the irate auctioneer descended upon us. Suffice to say that city pavements are notoriously hard and that our ardour for auctions was considerably dampened.

Some years elapsed before we ventured into the ranks again, but one fine day, motoring through a little village, we espied a crowd clustered in the front yard of a house. Once more the old thrill of an auction ensnared us. Good! There were two old chairs that were just what we needed for our hall at home. Now at that time our pocketbook was not very replete. (It still isn't, but it might be worse.) In fact it was best described as meagre, and all expenses were carefully budgeted. A hasty consultation, and it was agreed that we might go as high as fifteen dollars for the pair.

"We will now bid," said the auctioneer, lifting up one of "our" chairs, "on one of these chairs for the pair."

We opened up with a tentative bid. Someone promptly raised it. It took but a few minutes to reach and pass our limit of fifteen dollars. Throwing caution to the winds, we raised our bid. Finally, at twenty dollars victory was ours, and no other bid was heard in the land. To be sure, we had gone five dollars over our figure, but we could cut down on something else easily enough. Proudly we counted out the money and strode forth to gain the coveted prize. Alas, our joy was short-lived. "Forty dollars, please," said the unfeeling auctioneer. "I announced that we would bid on one for the pair." Alas, we had misconstrued his meaning entirely. Still, we didn't feel so badly when, happening to drop into one of the best known antique dealers in Philadelphia, we came across an identical pair of chairs priced at thirty-five dollars each.

Not long afterward we attended with our respected maternal parent the disposal of an estate whose owner, a bachelor of means, had long been a subject of much interest to the community and whose effects were said to be "naïve" and rather racy. Now the room was very warm, the auctioneer's voice very soothing; the Mater's head began nodding drowsily. But she came to with a start when she found that she had bid in a set of Boccaccio for seventy-five dollars!

Occasionally when in New York we drop in at the American Art Galleries or the Anderson Galleries to see what is going on, and we always

make a point of visiting our old friend, Jimmy
Silo, in his galleries on Vanderbilt Avenue. Seeing,
a few years ago, a grandfather's clock there that
struck our fancy, we left a bid, for we expected
to leave town before the sale. Something occurred
to prevent our departure, however, and recalling
the clock we dropped in on the sale. The bidding
was brisk, but finally it settled down to ourselves
and one other. Each time we'd raise the bid it
would be raised again. We looked about for our
opponent but could see him nowhere. Mystery
indeed. He seemed a determined fellow, but we
kept right on bidding until the auctioneer happened to look up and caught our eye. Bang! went
his gavel. "Sold!" he cried. "And it might interest
my friend," he added, "to know that he had been
bidding against himself for the last ten minutes."
We had completely forgotten our bid left with
him before the sale!

But of all the auctions—whether of books,
furniture, bric-à-brac, or anything else—the ones
we like best are cattle auctions. Maybe it is because they are a novelty to us or maybe because
we don't know anything about cows. But to
begin with they make a real event of a cattle
sale—a Field Day, as it were. One arrives early
and spends the morning examining prospective

purchases—much as they must have done in the slave marts of old. Then a halt is called at midday and a free lunch is served—a meal somewhat lacteal in character, to be sure, composed as it is largely of milk, butter, and cheese, and not the best thing for the figure, but delicious, just the same.

When the sale starts the fun begins. There is much excitement and much good-natured bidding. The auctioneer grows enthusiastic, and the cows, as they are led in, wax plaintive and express their astonishment at the proceedings with soft "moos." We grew so enthusiastic at one auction that we bid three hundred dollars for a cow and, what is more, for the space of three minutes actually owned the beast.

We must confess it was an agonizing three minutes, for while we like cows in the abstract, we, as we said before, know nothing about them. Furthermore, our facilities for housing, not to mention caring for, bossy were absolutely nil. To be sure we could park the Ford outside and install "Betsy Ross" or "Lulu Belle" or whatever the gentle creature was named, in the one-car garage, but even then a cow can't derive much nourishment from a diet of gasoline and waste.

So it was with a sigh of relief that we heard

our bid overtopped. Providence had been kind to us, and never again would we be rash enough to brave Fate that way. In fact, we have foresworn auctions from that day to this.

But time is a great healer. Life has been monotonous of late and we do need awfully a curly maple highboy for the bedroom. So we don't know—but—we—might—just—drop—down—some day—soon now and——

An Idyll of To-day

WE ARE afraid that under a cynical and morose exterior we are an incurable romanticist. We go to a play to scoff and remain to weep. The playing of an old familiar tune will cause us suddenly to blink furiously, and we're frankly fond of daydreaming. We enjoy the opera or a concert not so much for the music but for the mood it puts us in and for the opportunity it provides for our imagination to leave the dull routine of this mundane sphere and go skipping about at will, taking us, like the Magic Carpet, on the most fantastic voyages and weaving strange tales for our delectation. Furthermore, we regret to state that more often than not a sermon will put us into not entirely dissimilar mood.

It would seem with the passing of the years that our belief in the fulfilment of our dreams might have been shattered on the cruel rocks of reality. But every now and then some odd adventure—unexpected and entirely unlooked for—befalls us which seems to keep the spark of credulousness alive and once more looses the bonds of imagination.

Not long since we had such an experience—so enjoyable and so utterly charming as to be almost an idyll—if such things exist in the hurry and bustle of the Twentieth Century.

Now we've found in life that it is the spontaneous rather than the carefully planned event that has the true flavour of adventure and romance. So it was with our idyll. One summer day we set out, just two of us there were, on a small steamer for a short trip to an unknown—at least to us—island whose name sounded intriguing and of whose charms we had heard rumours—rumours which later proved well founded.

The harbour to our enchanted isle was so small that the steamer could not approach closely, and a speedy launch took us and our bags—for we had come but for a few days and were not en-

cumbered with impedimenta—to the green tree-
covered shore where we found ourselves in what
seemed another world. The hotel, shining white
in the almost tropical sun, was situated directly
on the harbour—a tiny body of turquoise blue
enclosed in two arms of a jetty that encircled it
and at whose end the red eye of a *phare* winked
at intervals through the night. From our window
was the loveliest view imaginable, and if we had
done nothing save gaze from the window the
trip would have been worth while.

But the cool green depths of the sea called to
us, so leisurely—it is a sin to hurry in Lotusland
—we found our way to the bathing pavilion
which like a Roman bath was set in a semicircle
on the shore front. How clear the depths of the
water, and how cool as we plunged into it. And
how delicious to lie on the raft and bask in the
warm rays of the sun. Later, how refreshing to
sit at one of the little tables under a gay little
umbrella by the waterside and sip an *apéritif* as
the sun slowly sank to rest. One evening just at
sundown we stole away on bicycles through fra-
grant groves of pine and cypress, passing Roman
ruins so old as to be almost prehistoric, and came
out suddenly on the rugged coast at the other
end of the island. How delicious it was, abandon-

ing our wheels, to plunge once more into the waters and swim up the lane of fire into the disappearing sun. Shelley would have made poetry of that!

Then back in the gathering dusk to dine by the side of the water, for the hotel boasted no dining room, and the tables were set in the open air in a semicircle right by the waterside. One night they held a festival. It was the Queen's birthday, they said. The little maids had been busy putting lighted candles in each of the hotel windows, and the yachts in the tiny harbour were brilliantly illuminated with strings of coloured lights. The effect was charming, and as we ate, a procession of gaily decorated and illuminated small boats wound its way over the waterside. The soft music of the guitars and the singing of the occupants were so beautiful as to render the scene almost unreal.

Later in the evening we danced—but not in a stuffy, ill-ventilated ballroom. No. As was fitting, we danced out under the stars in a grove of Pan. The floor we danced on was of pure marble, set in a semicircle and sunk below the level of the ground. Between dances we sat at small tables in the semicircle overlooking the dancing floor and sipped cooling drinks not sanctioned by Mr. Volstead. Overhead the moon cast her soft beams on the scene, and the whispering cypresses nodded among themselves in the scented breeze, casting long shadows on the couples gliding below. Do you wonder, then, that we lingered late and that Aurora dimmed the stars before we could leave the enchanted grove?

And do you wonder that we counted the hours spent on that happy island as blessed hours indeed? And do you wonder that we won't tell anyone where the magic isle is? For some day—some happy far-off day—we're going back. And we're going back reverently, hopefully, and perhaps just a little afraid—afraid, perchance, that some god, jealous of our idyll, may deny us such a gift a second time by turning loose hordes of swarming tourists to overrun our blessed isle.

Papa's reunion suit.

"Remember, Ma, you picked him out—I didn't!"

Motley

JUST what is it, we wonder, that prompts most mortals to a love for fancy dress? Just what urges ordinarily commonplace men and women to go into ecstasies at the thoughts of dressing in motley? Is it because man's everyday clothes are drear and drab? No, because the ladies like to dress up even more than the men, and their everyday raiment is far from drab. Is it a throwback to mediæval days when garments of both sexes were gay and giddy? Who knows? But whatever it is, it is an effective urge. It must be effective to cause thousands of members of our large fraternal orders to don silly looking fezzes and other quaint paraphernalia at their meetings. No doubt the Ku Klux Klan received a good deal of impetus from the fact that it called for a uniform, even though that uniform consisted largely of a sheet that sold for ten dollars or less.

Maybe it is because motley implies a sense of freedom. Costume parties are generally more unrestrained and hilarious than other parties where conventional dress clothes are worn.

Oddly enough, this love for uniform and fancy dress is in direct contradiction to the democratic principles of our nation. Witness the severe formal evening dress of our ambassadors and ministers at foreign court functions, which is in marked contrast to the gay uniforms and trappings of the other powers. Alexander Moore, our former ambassador to Spain, tells of one brilliant function in the Royal Palace at Madrid when their Majesties the King and Queen of Spain entertained the King and Queen of Italy. It was a truly brilliant spectacle, and one's eyesight was fairly dazzled by the splendour of the jewels and the uniforms of the guests. Alone the American ambassador stood out, a figure in solemn black. During the course of the evening the Queen asked the American ambassador if he did not think the spectacle a gorgeous one. Mr. Moore assented readily but added that there were two men who didn't seem to fit into the picture at all, in fact, would be more in place in the servants' hall. Perturbed, the Queen hastily inquired who the two offenders might be. "One is the King of Italy," drily remarked the American ambassador, "who is dressed like a chauffeur" (the Italian uniform is strangely like a chauffeur's livery) "and the other is myself, who is dressed like a head waiter."

Speaking of uniforms, have you ever attended a college reunion? If not, you have yet to realize what costuming really is. In the spring of the year Paterfamilias begins to assume an absent-minded air. His eye takes to roving and has a far-off vacant look. The experienced wife is not unduly alarmed. She knows the symptoms. Father's mind is turning back to good old days at Umpty Umph University. Already he can see the good old crowd foregathering for its 'steenth reunion. He can hear the good old chorus raised once again, and he can see himself in the vanguard of the parade proudly bearing the standard that proclaims to a waiting world why Oughty Ought is the greatest class Umpty Umph ever had.

And why shouldn't he daydream a bit? For months now his mail has consisted largely of appeals to make this the greatest reunion ever, supplemented by discreet suggestions as to a small check to assure the reunion's success. He has already sent in his measurements for his costume, which it is said will be a great surprise. And when he gets it it generally is. For somehow they must have mixed him up with the class baby. Well, anyway, the trousers will make a nice necktie.

The great day arrives, and he finds himself back in dear old Umpty Umph with the world forgotten for the next few days. Everyone, it seems, is in costume. There are pirates and Eskimos, sailors and toreadors, old, old men in striped blazers carrying Japanese parasols and young, young men as sheiks carrying transparencies having all sorts of humorous slogans such as "Four out of five have it and the fifth knows where to get it" or "Billy Sunday saved 300 girls. Who for?" Apaches stroll along with sailors, and hundreds of small children costumed in miniature are dragged mercilessly along by their progenitors. The costumes at first are gay and dapper, but after two or three days of continuous use, not to mention having in many cases been slept in, they lose much of their jauntiness. Mustard from hastily consumed hot dogs does not help things, and the last straw comes when a sudden thunderstorm drenches the mummers. Even then they won't relinquish the costumes. A reunion wouldn't be a reunion without costumes. And it is not until he is climbing aboard the train homeward bound, completely tired in mind and body, that Paterfamilias will relinquish his giddy apparel.

At that, from time to time during the coming month, he will furtively try on the coat or the hat, or possibly the whole suit, just to show Junior how Dad looked in the big parade. Right then and there Junior catches the germ. "Costumitis" has him in its grip, and when he grows to manhood he'll be ripe to join every organization that sports a gaudy uniform.

Oh, well, we suppose a love for motley is harmless, at least, and as a nation we must work off our surplus energy somehow.

"Yes, dear, it is very becoming to you."

What's in a Name?

THAT the question of bestowing a name upon a child or upon an inanimate object was a difficult one we knew, for after purchasing a small place in the country it was months, almost a year, before we hit upon a name that was, at least to us, at all suitable. But that nomenclature could be raised to the dignity of an actual business, even a profession, was new to us. Yet such is the case, for only the other day in a magazine we came across the advertisement of a young lady who called herself a nomenclator and announced to a waiting world that she was prepared for a suitable sum to find an appropriate name for everything from triplets to a country house, Pullman cars only excepted. Intrigued, we went to call upon her, and the hour we passed with her was well spent.

Babies, she assured us, were easy enough because if one delved through family archives long enough one would be sure to find a suitable name.

We were inclined to be skeptical. Having la-
boured all our life under a distinct handicap as to
our own name, and having passed a rather gory,
embattled childhood for this same cause, we were
inclined to think that the reason naming babies
was easy was that the unfortunate infants
couldn't retaliate. And in naming a child think
what a gamble you take! How many delicate
little Graces have you seen grow up into strapping
Amazons? And what of the candy-loving, pil-
low-like Lilies that meet one on every side? Why,
the toughest boy in our school was named Clar-
ence. To pursue the subject further, a doctor
friend of ours had as one of his patients in the
charity ward of a Baltimore hospital a little
Italian boy who had among other things bow legs,
curvature of the spine, a hare lip, and other afflictions too numerous to mention—and the placard
at the head of the bed proudly announced the
fact that the poor lad's name was Fortunatus!
Yet the nomenclator (candidate for the realtor
and mortician clubs) assured us that naming
children was easy.

If children are easy, what of Pullman cars and
ferry boats? How many times have you travelled
on the Oxwotamie or the Geiferdown or the
Nitzipooka? How could you ever hope to recall

such names if you happened to leave something behind in a sleeper or parlour car? And have you ever crossed on the good old ferry boat the *Secaucus* or the *Musconnetcong,* both of which may still be ploughing the waters of the Hudson River for all we know?

Naming places, we are informed, requires a little more thought. The nomenclator's method is first to look about and see if the place has any natural features to suggest a name—like Rocking Stone Farm or White Birches. But again there is danger. We had a friend who called his country home Tamarack Top because of a lovely tamarack that grew by his door. A worthy idea, no doubt, but alas, within a year a bolt of lightning shattered the tamarack and our friend had to start all over again. Similarly, another friend who bought a farm in the spring called it Stony Brook only to have the brook dry up in a few weeks. And where are the Forests or the Hills in Forest Hills, N. Y.? And wherever did they get Hollywood from?

In case there is no natural feature a good idea —we paraphrase the nomenclator—is to try to combine the owner's names. Therefore, if Alice and John own a place you might make "Aljo" or "Joal"—or what have you? We tried this scheme on an unfortunate pair of friends whose place is still, after many years, nameless. By many permutations and combinations we triumphantly combined their names to form "Harl-em." But somehow they didn't seem extra pleased with it.

Or you might just try writing names backward. This is the school that has produced "Acirema" in such vast quantities, so we cannot really urge you to try it. And for heaven's sake don't be influenced by the Ku Klux Klan to call your camp "Kamp Kill Kare."

But there are any quantity of aptly named places. We recall particularly Upsan Downs for a hilly estate, and Dunmovin needs no comment. Planting Fields, Clover Fields, County Line Farm, Greentree, Appledowns, Beaverwood Hollow, are apt and charming. But why Blink Bonnie or Drumthwacket, two actual names that we recall?

Heaven help you if you have a tea room to christen. You'll need all the imagination you've got to keep away from the Dewdrop Inns, Stumble Inns, Duck Inns, Drop Inns, Always Inns, and Kum Inns that dot the landscape. Still, a trip along the Boston Post Road in summer will convince you that there are some prettily named ones. For instance, the Old Wishing Well Tea Room, outside of Lyme, Conn., is as quaint and aptly named as you could wish, and the Old Mill, at Roslyn, L. I., is happily christened.

When it comes to naming pets one's imagination seems more fertile. Edward Hope, the "colyumist" of the New York *Herald Tribune,* aptly calls his little dog Molly Cule, and a big gray disdainful tomcat in our neighbourhood rejoices in the appropriate title of Emperor Jones. In our youth we had a fat little white pony whom we called Mallow. The point of the name was that it was a little French Canadian pony and the French Canadian term for "giddap" is "marche" (marsh). So you can imagine our infantile delight as we perched on the dashboard and shouted, "Marche-Mallow." Christopher Morley would have enjoyed that!

When it comes to names of towns, especially in the East, our ancestors seem to have been particularly unimaginative. Possibly it was the Puritanical complex at work, or they were tired after the long tempestuous trip overseas, or maybe it was on account of homesickness that they named so many places after spots in the homeland. Who can tell! But Rome, Athens, Paris, etc., all seem so out of place in our new civilization. And there are so many unlovely names. Take Smithtown or Hicksville on Long Island. What does it matter that they honour the memory of sturdy pioneers long since deceased? How much better to have kept the old Indian names. And yet Hicksville held a plebiscite to consider changing the name of the town, and voted to retain the old name.

Each section of the country seems to have its distinctive names. Charleston, Annapolis, Baltimore—the very names have an aristocratic sound that bespeaks the splendour of the old days of stately country mansions just as in the Province of Quebec every other town is named after a saint—St. Joachim, St. Eustache, St. Onesime— that tells of the enduring faith and piety of the French Canadian peasant. But the best named towns of all are those that have retained the original Indian name or its English equivalent. Take Tallahassee or Osceola or Winona or Manitou or Okeechobee—not only are the names pretty in themselves, but they possess a quality of romance. And what legends gather round such spots as Klondike, Big Horn, Medicine Hat, Moosejaw, Saskatchewan, Red Cloud, Cheyenne, and hosts of other names too numerous to mention. Sometime when you're on a long journey and the trip begins to pall, dig into the time-tables and study some of the names you see dotted across the length and breadth of this great land of ours. It's a fine lesson in history and geography all rolled in one, and beats that old train game of roadside cribbage all hollow.

We would urge you to do this, especially if you are in the real estate business, for surely the prize for foolish names must be awarded to the real estate gentry who have taken to bestowing the most fanciful names upon unpretentious developments in the hope of ensnaring a gullible public. We call to mind particularly Robinwood for a flat sandy stretch; Sunrise Terrace for a bleak plain; Marmaduke Estates, a No Man's Land on the outskirts of a great city; and countless Treasure and Pleasure Lands. More sacrifices to the great god Bunk.

Yes, this business of naming is a great game but beset with difficulties. Yet there are aids to solve your problem, no doubt, for witness this clipping from *Our Sunday Visitor*—a weekly published in Kansas:

> LISTEN! Pretty names for your baby. Over 500 names to select from. 50 cents.
> WEBB EGBERT, CIMARRON, KANSAS.

No trouble at all to name the baby, and at what trifling cost. We haven't a baby to name, alas, at this present juncture, but forewarned is forearmed; and anything to get away from the avalanche of Sheilas that seems to be sweeping the land. Yes, we think we'll risk fifty cents, and it has just occurred to us that if we had sent for the list before starting to write this screed it would probably have been much more interesting. We'll wager there are some priceless cognomens in the list.

"But you said last week the price was only four hundred dollars!"

"Yes, but it got busted up a lot more in an accident since then and that makes it a lot antiquer."

Concerning Antiques

ANTIQUES, we confess, are to us, at least, like olives, an acquired taste. We can remember when we used to look upon the collecting of antiques with the utmost scorn and wonder why on earth people should give good money for rickety old chairs and sofas when they could easily purchase brand-new ones that wouldn't give way or creak dismally when anyone sat in them. We can remember our complete surprise when one of our friends who was about to be married expressed a desire for gifts of antique furniture. We simply couldn't understand her delight and her joy in antiques.

To-day we know better. We have completely succumbed. We are not in any sense a collector, yet we love the old things. Just how or when this change came about we are totally unable to tell. We think it must have been a gradual evolution. We strongly suspect that Alice Van Leer Carrick had a great deal to do with it, for she was always so vastly entertaining about her pet theme and had so many anecdotes to tell of her experiences. Anyway, we felt that we had gained the highest honour in the land when she addressed to us one of her collector's letters from England, which were published in *House Beautiful*. So you can see how completely under the spell of the antique we have fallen. And you can realize how bitterly we regret, to-day, that this love did not come to us earlier, when we lived in the midst of a veritable gold mine of antiques and never realized it. The old adage *"Si jeunesse savait, si vieillesse pouvait"* never held more true than in our case.

We remember Grandfather's big house where we all lived when we were youngsters. It had a wonderful attic with lots of quaint and eerie ells and crannies, and it was full almost to bursting with all manner of old trunks and furniture that had been accumulated with the passing of the years. There came a day while we were still very young, when the old house was sold and everything in it had to be removed in a great hurry. Haste was imperative, and there was no time to pause and determine the value of things stored in the old attic. Even to-day, years afterward, we shudder when we think of the holocaust that

took place. First editions without number were
consigned forthwith to the junk heap. Complete
files of the early numbers of magazines like *Life*
and *Punch* were given to the butcher boy or anyone who would take them. Trunks full of old
letters were burned without qualms; the stamps
alone on them, such as the early issues of "Boyd's
City Dispatch," etc., would have brought quite
a small fortune to-day. Furniture was sold by
lots for what it would bring and the attic cleared
out as fast as possible. Of course, not all of it was
good. Not even most of it, probably, for there
was a vast amount of ugly Victoriana in the lot for
which the junk heap was the proper repository,
but still the mind loves to speculate on what
might have been.

But it's no use to think of what might have
been; with thousands of others we've learned to
love the good old furniture and to begin collecting. Now our collecting must necessarily be a
long and slow process, for two reasons: first and
most important, the smallness of the exchequer;
and secondly, lack of time. We envy Lurelle Guild
and Sally Lockwood and Alice Carrick, those
inveterate antiquers, who seem to have ample
time to dash about hunting the elusive antique
and turning the hunt into actual dollars and

cents. It is a positive gift, and you'll find the strangest sort of people famous as collectors. One man that we know, who is a most successful insurance agent, is an even more successful collector of early American glass. Then there is a famous Labour leader who undoubtedly has the best collection of Bennington pottery in America. It is these contrasts, combined with the gambler's lure of always hoping to uncover treasure which has long been hidden, that make collecting the fascinating sport it is.

We have our favourite antiquarian who has a most fascinating little shop. Never mind just where; we don't want the world beating a path to his door, nor does he, for that matter, for he has quite enough to attend to now, and money holds no great charm for him. His little shop, with a window full of all manner of things that would have delighted the heart of Charles Dickens, lies on the road to our office—a fateful (and a costly) situation for us, we fear. Rarely a day goes by but we stop in to see the Major, and rarely a day goes by but the Major has heard of some wonderful bargain that is one's for almost the asking. And they generally are bargains, too, for the Major knows and loves his business. You can't deceive him, and he won't deceive you.

Antiques are at once his joy and his livelihood, and he is content to sit back among his treasured possessions and let time's grains of sand run slowly from the hourglass. We got to stopping at the Major's store so regularly that we had to call a halt. It became for us a daily event, like going to the butcher's or the grocer's. So now we don't visit the antiquarian as much as we'd like to, but there's always a treat in store for us when we do.

What amazes us, in this present craze, is the search for and the sale of articles that really have no intrinsic worth or beauty. There are a great many Currier & Ives prints that are really unlovely, the comics especially, and we refuse to consider Rogers groups as real antiques. We confess to a liking for those glass globes inclosing a church or a ship, in which by shaking one can create a miniature snowstorm—in fact, we have one before us as we write—and we even have a penchant for those pressed glass butter dishes in the form of a hen seated on a basket that were so prevalent twenty or thirty years ago. Silhouettes and samplers too are favourites of ours, but the real delights are the graceful pieces of furniture of Phyfe and Hepplewhite and Sheraton, or the banjo clocks of Simon Willard. And what is lovelier than the old pewter of our grandfathers or the chaste silver of Paul Revere? In these one finds the full flavour of the antique at its best, and it is due to their beauty that we are alive and awake to the charm and the loveliness that lie in the genuine antique.

"Look, dearie, I've just bought the darlingest what-not wreck and it only cost a mortgage on our income for the next seven weeks!"

"nnng!"

Stamps 'n' Maps 'n' Everything

WE'VE just had another illusion shattered. One of our fondest hopes has gone a-glimmering. We've discovered, after nursing for many years a secret desire to become a full-fledged philatelist, that stamps and stamp collecting no longer interest us. The dénouement came about in this way. As a youngster we were an ardent collector of stamps; we begged, borrowed, or "swapped," as we called it, stamps with the greatest enthusiasm. We'd spend whole days pasting our treasures in great brown-covered stamp albums, and we were assiduous readers of a weekly stamp journal, *Meckel's Weekly Stamp News*, if we remember rightly. For several years our allowance was rigidly saved up until we had sufficient funds to purchase a Cape of Good Hope Triangular stamp or an entire page of a Honduras issue, which oddly enough were more costly cancelled than new. We can even remember stooping so low as trying to borrow the village postmaster's cancelling machine in order to cancel a set of these same stamps which, owing to a lack of funds, we had been forced to purchase in their pristine state.

One of the greatest inducements to collecting stamps we felt was the fact that, unlike so many other youthful pastimes, stamp collecting could be indulged in throughout one's life. For were not the King of England and many other famous grown-ups assiduous collectors? Then, too, we felt that stamps were a good investment, although this idea was somewhat rudely shaken when a friend of ours, who had spent hundreds of dollars on his collection (a vast sum to our eyes, grown used to an allowance of fifty cents a week), disposed of it for a little more than four dollars. But we hung on to our collection with its chief prize, an odd-shaped stamp marked "Boyd's City Dispatch," and continued our joyful visits to that mecca of stamp collectors, the Scott Stamp & Coin Company.

But as we grew older, spare time grew less and less. Gradually we put our stamp collection away and referred to it but rarely. Ten years went by without our so much as looking at it. But always we felt that it was merely a temporary abandonment. The day would come when we should have more leisure, and then we'd return to our old love.

A visit to Paris and a view of the open-air stamp market under the trees of the Champs Élysées one year aroused old memories, and when a great International Stamp Exhibit was announced we hurried to it gleefully. Alas! It would have been better had we stayed away. Our idol came crashing earthward! For to be perfectly truthful the rows upon rows of stamps bored us beyond words. We tried to summon the old enthusiasm. In vain. We gazed long and keenly at the dark-hued octagon stamp from British Guiana that cost $22,000 and was said to be the only one of its kind in the world. We were unimpressed. Sorrowfully we tottered from the hall, a disillusioned and broken being.

But Fate after all is kindly. Though a career in philately be closed to us, we've acquired—along with a million other people, apparently—a growing fondness for old maps. They've become almost a hobby with us. An expensive one but no more expensive than stamps were in proportion in the early days. The old maps are so quaint and fascinating, and their pursuit nowadays, when everyone is so eagerly seeking them out, is a fascinating sport. It seems a pity that so many of the lovely old atlases are being torn ruthlessly apart and the

maps sold individually or being used for all manner of decorative purposes by interior decorators.
For you'll find maps to-day adorning the oddest
sorts of places. You'll see them on scrap baskets,
blotters, ash trays, pen wipers, match boxes, umbrella stands, and the Lord knows what; and of
course they make really very lovely lampshades.
In fact, they run Godey prints, old hunting
scenes, and the pages cut from ancient missals a
close race for first place in modern decoration.
And yet the only place for these maps is the atlases in which they were bound. Don't imagine
for one moment that we are decrying the artistic
value of maps or their use in decoration. Certainly nothing could be lovelier than the gaily
coloured maps on the walls of the Galleria Geo-
grafica in the Vatican at Rome, or the lovely
maps in the Uffizi Palace in Florence. Here they
fullfil the purpose for which they were intended.
And our modern artists, quick to sense the charm
of maps similarly employed, have used them to
distinct advantage in our modern homes and office
buildings. What could be lovelier than the mural
maps of Barry Faulkner, Arthur Covey, and Fred
Dana Marsh? And for the decorating of the
library or the overmantel in the dining room or
for the business office, there is nothing more de-

lightful than those modern maps, done in the old style that Major Ernest Clegg is executing.

But for real enjoyment of maps go some day to the library of your town and ask to see some of the old atlases. What quaint conceptions of the world old cartographers had. What an unknown quantity the world at large must have been to them. Their ideas, to say the least, were rudimentary, much like what our ideas of the universe itself must be to-day.

Naturally the New World was *terra incognita* to them, and they peopled it with all manner of strange beasts and people. The seas are filled with sea serpents in fabulous coils, and whales—but the strangest looking whales. Evidently the early voyagers confused walruses and whales, for we see the latter pictured with a whale's head, body, and tail—generally in the act of spouting—but possessing great tusks, bushy whiskers, fierce eyes, and prominent ears. One map—not very rare—has a scene showing beavers as large as lions and more like the latter in appearance than like beavers, busily employed in cutting down trees in a vain effort to dam Niagara Falls, apparently.

But on another and much rarer map we found even stranger four-footed animals, obviously carnivorous, for they were earnestly engaged in consuming unfortunate natives or sailors from visiting ships. What made these animals unusually interesting was the fact that in the middle of the back they carried what was evidently a square chimney out of which black smoke was belching. Some day, when we've more time, we are going back and dig out just what manner of beasties these were, for the caption did not say.

A final and extremely useful employment of maps to-day is gaining favour among our country friends. That is the idea of having a map made of the best roads to reach their house from the nearest large city. Anyone who has ever set out to find a friend's house in the country, especially at night, by automobile, knows what a struggle it is to find it and will appreciate immensely the receipt of such a little map, either as a card at Christmas time—or any other time, for that matter. It is an idea that we should like to see taken up to a greater extent by all our country friends who care to see us.

"officer, can you direct me to the zoo?"

"sure! it's just under my shoulder blade."

A traffic cop with map-embroidered uniform.

On the Trail of Spring

SPRING, it is generally conceded, is the peculiar, almost exclusive, property of poets. These long-haired flowing-tied gentry from time immemorial have been considered the only mortals gifted enough really to appreciate gentle spring. Since those early days, and considerably before, when Chaucer struck his plaintive note and sang of

April with his shoures sote

the bards have never failed to greet the earth's renaissance with bursts of joyous song. Now we are not a poet; we know little or nothing about meter, yet we defy anyone to find a greater enthusiast about Spring than ourself. In fact, sometimes we've grown so impatient of waiting that we've deliberately anticipated her coming and stolen a march by appointing ourself a sort of welcoming committee and going South to greet the vernal

season. One year we had four springs. We left
the snow and ice of the North and found Spring
dallying in the soft sunshine of Florida. We followed her to South Carolina and witnessed her
gorgeous, truly triumphal entry in the flaming
colours of the lovely Magnolia Gardens at Charleston. Then we sped North in time to greet her in
the lush meadows and cool greens of Pennsylvania
and New York. Finally, at a time when Summer
had usurped her throne everywhere else, we pursued elusive Spring and caught up with her in
a riot of apple blossoms in the lovely orchards of
New England and Canada.

Of all the joys that Spring brings, two are
uppermost in our mind: First, the return of the
flowers; and second, the return of the birds. How
thrilling one morning to wander through the
woods, where patches of snow still linger, and
come upon a sturdy gay little band of snowdrops
poking their heads through the very snow itself.
And how gorgeous to find later the very ground
carpeted with the golden glow of myriads of daf-
fodils. The cup of life is full indeed then. But
even lovelier than this is it to be awakened at dawn
by the soft twitterings of the birds in the trees.
How delicious it is to lie abed and listen to their
chirpings while the rosy sun climbs slowly over

the neighbouring hill and gilds the landscape with her lovely pastels, and all the while the bird music swells and grows as the light grows stronger and stronger. Here indeed is heavenly satisfaction as nearly perfect as it can be on this mundane sphere of ours.

Lately we'll admit that Spring has disappointed us greatly. Winter has come and alas! Spring has been far, far behind. The seasons, they tell us, are changing. We wonder. True, it has been almost June on several occasions before the weather really turned warm but somehow we cannot believe that they have really changed. Spring has only dallied a bit too long for several successive years. But that is all. She is really still doing business at the old stand, only she has been a little slow in taking down the blinds. But one thing is certain, when she does come she is always welcome and our enthusiasm for her arrival has not diminished one whit with the passing of the years.

Were it not for a mournful note, an inexplicable feeling of melancholy about Autumn, we should be inclined to give her second place in our choice of the seasons. Even with this handicap we are almost inclined to award her the red ribbon, but then we think of emerald lakes, shining like jewels under a summer sun, of cool green

forests swaying in soft winds, and of long stretches
of sandy beaches with the waves breaking joyously upon them, and we come to the conclusion
that after all Summer should and does rank second in our estimation. What can compare with
the feel of blue water surging along your keel
as the white-winged boat dances softly over the
waves? And for sheer contentment what could
be more enjoyable, more peaceful, than the
drowsy contentment of a summer day at high
noon, when the locusts shrill in the fields and the
soft noise of the haymakers comes to our ears on
the flower-scented breeze? And what of the delights of a plunge into green waters or the joy
of whipping a tumbling brook with your
favourite light-weight rod? All the world's at
peace then, and all the world's at play. But
Autumn has its compensations. The first cool day
brings an exhilaration to senses dulled by the
warmth of Summer. Your nerves are atingle and
your spirits high. And where can one find a more
lovely season than our Autumn in America? Long
days with the atmosphere so clear it almost hurts.
Every detail of the landscape stands out as if
each part had been newly scrubbed and washed.
Great fleecy white clouds etch themselves against
the deep blue of heaven, and as we watch the

landscape changes colour. The deep yellows and red replace the tired greens of summer. Here and there a maple flashes scarlet against the russet yellow of the meadow, while the sumac and the Virginia creeper make a living frame against the sombre colours of the woods. The katydids are at their noisiest and the field mice and squirrels are busy with their winter stores.

In the orchards the fruit trees bend under their loads. Great clusters of apples, Pippins, Baldwins, Pound Sweets, all the fruits of the orchard, weigh down the branches until they have to be supported or break under the sheer weight of their burden. In the valley the cider mill is at work overtime and everywhere there is a cheerful bustle and hurry to set everything to rights before Jack Frost puts an end to activities.

And so we come to Winter. Even though it be generally conceded the least attractive of the seasons, there are many who would disagree with any such statement. Winter, particularly in the country, is a time of calm and content. There is not much work to be done. One has time to pause and reflect, and cheerful evenings before an open fire, while the wind roars and howls around the house, is an experience not to be despised. And what of the youngsters? They have always hailed Winter as their own. A piece of black ice and a pair of skates spell contentment and health. A snowy hillside and a pair of skis mean rosy cheeks and sunny smiles. And don't forget the moonlight nights, when the earth lies motionless and silent under its great mantle of white, while overhead the stars twinkle with renewed brilliance and the Aurora sends her trembling wavy beams across the dark vault of heaven. Most of us have yet really to discover the joy of our winters, but each year finds hundreds of new devotees turning northward rather than south as the cold waxes. Yes, Winter has its compensations, but ho-hum! Spring is just around the corner—and well, after all, you just can't expect us to be exactly downcast about it, now, can you?

The Same Old Christmas

CHRISTMAS, they tell us, has lost its significance. It has become too commercialized and the giving and receiving of presents is stressed too much. We don't believe it for a minute. No doubt they said the same thing fifty or a hundred or even a thousand years ago. Furthermore, we don't want to believe it, and if we don't want to, why should we? Probably the people who go around pulling long faces and decrying the loss of the Christmas spirit are the same group from whom we've heard so much in recent years about the younger generation going to the demnition bow-wows and worse. We're tired of this cry of "Wolf, wolf." As far as we can see, the younger generation if anything is better than its predecessors. What if they are a little more outspoken and frank than the youngsters of the Elsie book era; who, in heaven's name, wouldn't have it so? And as for

Christmas—why it seems to us that Christmas grows to mean more and more each year. Look at the widespread charity that is bestowed each Christmas Day upon our less fortunate fellow men, and the spread of the idea of exchanging gifts among friends certainly would indicate increased unselfishness.

Furthermore, we seem to be reverting, as far as it is possible in our complex civilization of to-day, more and more to the traditional celebration of the day, with its elaborate heartfelt ceremonies that our forefathers indulged in.

Yes, Christmas to-day for us is every bit as enjoyable as it was when we were a youngster, and we still like to celebrate it in the old-fashioned way. We have seen many Christmas Days in our times, some enjoyable, others—from unavoidable circumstances—perhaps not so much so, but along the highway of life some of these Christmas milestones are brighter than others. Particularly do we remember the long-gone Christmas dinners in the big, stately old house of our grandmother. Here was an event we looked forward to for weeks, more eagerly awaited, perhaps, than Santa Claus and his well-filled stockings. For weeks we practised diligently in honour of the occasion, learning a good old carol or some appropriate

verse, to burst upon an appreciative and we trust
—but from a vantage point of later years, doubt
—delighted audience of grown-ups.

What preparations there were for the great
event. How we were scrubbed and brushed and
thrust into that most torturous, thoroughly
hated, and wholly uncomfortable garment, an
Eton suit. When finally all the family had assembled and had been greeted as politely as we
knew how, the doors of the dining room were
thrown open and we trooped in. Surely Paradise
could be as nothing compared with this! Those
were happy days indeed, and we shall never fail
to regret their inevitable passing as Time slowly
turned the scroll of the years.

Quite different but equally poignantly remembered was our first Christmas away from home.
Fresh from delightful but somewhat sheltered
academic walls of learning, we had, a few weeks
before the holiday season, taken a position in a
lumber mill in a tiny hamlet in the Far North.
Buried under a mantle of snow, the inhabitants
strove to make merry as best they could; but we,
a stranger, knowing no one, must needs pass
Christmas alone. We woke early and hastened
out to early service. Cold gray skies and whirling
snowflakes greeted us. Service over, we hurried

home, stopping at the post office to inquire eagerly for mail. For the family had warned us that we were not forgotten and that a box of good things had been sent us. But the postmaster was adamant; no mail had come for us or anyone else, and he was quite right. Nothing had. Somewhere on the bleak line of the Quebec and Lake St. John Railway our Christmas box was held up by unfeeling snowdrifts. Dismally we ate breakfast. Seeking companionship, we brought the neighbour's dog in to bear us company. He had been lying quietly at our feet while we read a week-old newspaper for no more than ten minutes, when he suddenly raised his muzzle and gave vent to a series of long-drawn-out and utterly desolate howls. A furtive kick and he went flying, while we sought comfort and oblivion by going back to bed and drowning our sorrows in sleep.

But perhaps the best Christmas of all and one that we recall the most vividly was a sort of Dickensian one in the gray old city of Quebec. On the heels of a young blizzard we arrived on Christmas Eve, and when we were awakened next morning by all the chimes in the world, it seemed, the city was a shimmering mass of white. We were up early, too, for we were to partake of a typically Pickwickian breakfast. What a repast it was! Just like those you see in the old prints. Cold meats, hot meats, Melton Mowbray pies, venison, and pheasant—here they all were in gorgeous array upon the table, and all this for breakfast. We set to with a will; later we wished that we hadn't. We left our hospitable host only to hurry to another friend's house for the midday meal. Here another gastronomic masterpiece awaited us. There were oysters creamed and oysters raw, sausages, fowl of every kind and description, potted meats and salads galore, mince pies and plum puddings on every side, and all washed down with copious draughts of ale and wine. Now Quebec is noticeably a city of hills and declivities. Furthermore, it was very cold and very, very slippery. So when we set out to visit the next friend's house for tea, is it any wonder that we found our footing unstable and an occasional snowbank a very warm and a very comfortable place to rest and compose one's thoughts in?

Tea, high tea—very high, in fact—was another epicurean ambush for the unwary. Again tables groaning under weight of good things. Our eyes grew glassy at the sight of food, but the worst was yet to come, for the climax of the day was the Christmas dinner that night. We have a hazy recollection of a very formal affair, great expanses of white shirt fronts and much silver and plate. We don't know—never will know, in fact —just how many courses there were; we lost count after the eighth, but another Christmas Day had been safely stowed away in the archives of Time before we left the festive board.

Yes, an English Christmas is a wonderful institution. We are heartily in favour of it, at a distance, but if you must needs have such a celebration, a word of warning—start training well in advance for it. And it might not be a bad plan to refrain from eating anything much for a week or so before, because you certainly won't eat much for a week afterward, and crackers and milk are an acquired taste, after all.

Trophies

THE other day we paid a visit to our attic. It was a rainy day and there was no possibility of pottering around the place, pruning a tree or two or waging battle against the ubiquitous tent caterpillar. To be sure we had hauled out the long ladder and poked a kerosene torch into the middle of one or two caterpillar tenements; but the rain in our face soon dampened our ardour, and we put the torch away and went indoors. We opened up the trap door of the attic and began browsing around. An old trunk caught our fancy first. We lifted from the top of the trunk the pile of framed photographs —groups of high-school days, football teams, debating clubs, etc.—all the fascinating paraphernalia of our bygone days relegated to the nether regions by stern edict of the real head of the household. One by one we stopped to examine the prints and to "turn our memory back" so that by the time we opened the trunk we were in the proper mellow mood for reflection.

The tray was full of all manner of things so we sat down to examine it more closely. Soon we came upon several silver mugs badly tarnished and a loving cup or two. There were also one or two medals hanging on frayed ribbons—symbols of athletic glory long since departed. Mournfully we looked at our growing waistline and wondered how it could ever have been, and sadly we mused at the low state into which our trophies, once so highly prized and proudly displayed, had fallen. At that, though, there was no denying that the cups and medals were not things of beauty, and so far as utility was concerned they were negligible. Here no doubt was the answer. Had they been beautiful or even useful they would have been with us to-day instead of languishing upstairs in an old trunk. The subject opened up possibilities. We recalled other similar instances.

An uncle of ours, a great whip in his day, had showcase after showcase filled with prize ribbons won by his horses. For years after his death they were the white elephant of the family, until finally the advent of the modern apartment with its low ceilings forced their disposal on the dump heap despite the reverential attitude of the family for these glories long since departed.

Then there was an aunt, also, who for years had one of the finest strings of show horses in the country. Each year these beauties made the circuit of all the horse shows, collecting trophy after trophy as they went, until finally the walls of one large room were almost completely hidden behind the rows of cups that adorned them. Yet what happened in the natural course of events? The stable was dispersed and the trophies were disposed of for what they would bring.

Quite recently we have learned of a movement that seems a splendid one and worthy of encouragement. It is to do away with the dispensing of the unæsthetic and useless cup as a prize trophy, substituting in its stead a suitable bronze statue or a bas relief or even an etching or a painting. What a relief such a movement would be to the average household, and of what incalculable benefit to the growing boy or girl in getting them to take pride in owning a really fine piece of art by some famous sculptor or etcher. Let us hope that the idea will be universally adopted—the sooner the better. In all humbleness we might venture to suggest that a good place to begin would be by scrapping the *America's* Yacht Cup, that monstrosity of curves and furbelows, and substitute a really artistic trophy; and while we are about it, an æsthetic substitute for the Davis Cup for international lawn tennis would not be so difficult to find.

Now, while we were poking about the attic we stumbled over a deer's head that we had shot as a boy and which in time had found its way to the attic. Sadly dilapidated and showing the ravages of hungry moths, it was really a pathetic spectacle of a once proud head. That set us to thinking again. Of what use, anyway, are stuffed animal heads, whether they are of moose or of rhinoceros? They are nothing but symbols of overweening vanity, and we have yet to see the room whose appearance was improved by either stuffed fish or stuffed animals. How much better, if one must preserve the wild things, to do it with a camera. One can get just as much of a thrill out of studying their habits at close range as by shooting them. We admit that in our day we have shot game. Frankly, not with much success. Being nearsighted we wounded so many animals that we feared lest the local S. P. C. A. prosecute us. As we grew older, however, we learned wisdom. Live and let live is our motto now, and we've put away the gun forever.

The uselessness of the slaughter was brought
home to us a few years ago when a friend with
whom we were hunting killed a fine moose. We
skinned the animal on the spot, and the guides
staggered home under the load of the tremendous
head. My friend wrestled with the hide, while
to us was assigned the task of carrying the steaks
the long way to the base camp. Never would we
have believed it possible for moose steaks to weigh
so much. They were more like cannon balls.
Eventually we reached our goal more dead than
alive! Alas, in a day or so, when we went to eat
the steak, we found that the blow flies had gotten
into them and they were unfit for food. Later,
when we sent the hide to be tanned, all the hair
on it fell out; and finally, when after months
the head, beautifully mounted, arrived from the
taxidermist's, it seemed so out of place in any
room in the house that it was promptly relegated
to the barn, where no doubt it still reposes, if
it has not disintegrated under the dust of the
passing years.

Another useless sacrifice we recall was when we
shot a small bear. We won't go into the embarrassing details as to how we happened to hit and
kill the animal. Suffice to say that we had actually
accomplished what to our adolescent mind was

an extraordinary feat. In due course the bear's skin reached the taxidermist and, becoming a warm rug, was put beside the bed in our room. Alas, happening to be absent for a short visit, the rug was borrowed for some amateur theatricals, where it added local colour to a scene in a log cabin. That was the last we ever saw of it. It disappeared mysteriously at the end of the performance, and searching and questioning never revealed its whereabouts. So poor Bruin had been sacrificed in vain.

Let us hope that prize cups, stuffed animals, and all the other useless and unlovely trophies will soon be a thing of the past and that a few years more will find them relegated to that limbo where the cast-iron deer and the Rogers groups patiently await them.

"hurry, car, you're too slow!"

put-put-put-

TEMPUS

Another Milestone Left Behind

WE'VE just passed another milestone on the road of life and we're extremely pleased. No, not on having had a birthday; we are no more anxious to be older, thank you, than anyone else is. (Though we can remember when we were so anxious to be thought older than we were that we actually grew a moustache so that the boss would take us more seriously and raise our pay. Now we're considering shaving the darn thing off for, oddly enough, the same reason.)

But our cause for rejoicing this time is that the festive natal day came and went without any of our numerous relatives and few friends remembering it. For if there is one thing we hate to be reminded of it is our advancing years, and telegrams of congratulations—we almost said condolence, which would be more appropriate—are so much gall and wormwood in our mouth. Not that we are ashamed of our years and finding life a dull, drab thing. On the contrary, pollyanna-wise we find almost every year better than the last, but we hate to have the actual rounding of the buoy thrown in our face, as it were.

We are guilty of a slight inaccuracy, however, when we say that no one remembered our birth-day. There are two people who, come what may, never forget to send us greetings on the fatal day. One of these we could easily dispense with, for we suspect—in fact we know—that the greeting rises from commercial motives. The greeting, as you may have guessed, comes from our life insurance agent.

We should feel strangely uneasy and disappointed if we failed to receive the other greeting. Yet oddly it comes from thousands of miles away, and we have never seen nor do we ever expect to see the sender, for it comes from the leper settlement in the Hawaiian Islands.

You all know Father Damien, the heroic martyr priest who spent and gave his life for the lepers at Molokai. When he died some thirty years or more ago he was succeeded by one of his helpers, Brother Joseph Dutton, who since that day has never left Hawaii and his charges and says he never will. A valiant soldier of the Lord, Brother Dutton is a member of the G. A. R. and fought throughout the Civil War with the Union Forces. Although in the eighties, he carries on his work among his leper charges without ever losing touch with or interest in the world at large, and the United States in particular, which he loved so well in his youth. We came in contact by correspondence with Brother Dutton while serving with the Red Cross during the war, and since that time we have become a firm friend and a great admirer of Brother Dutton. Somehow the latter learned the date of our birthday, and since 1919 he has never failed to send us a word of greeting and so perfectly timed that it arrives almost invariably on the day itself. Do you wonder, then, that this is the one birthday remembrance we look forward to eagerly and which we would miss more than we care to say should it fail to arrive?

But it was not always so with us. There was a time when a birthday was second only to Christmas, to our way of thinking. It was as eagerly anticipated, and the night before was just as sleepless as Christmas Eve. An unfortunate family was roused somewhere near dawn, and all the long day we held sway, our word law for the once and our wishes promptly obeyed (that is, within reason). Generally we'd elect to spend the day on the water, and what a joyous hegira on the waters of Narragansett Bay we would have, with a birthday cake in the cabin of the little launch hired for the day from our friend, Captain Champion. What mattered it though the floor was slippery from the scales of the mackerel we'd caught, or that one of the fair members of the party would almost faint (this was the mauve decade, you see) when she'd pull in a hideous grimacing skate instead of a placid old flounder.

Then, later on, when for many years we'd given up the nautical cruises, we'd elect to invite all our young friends to a dance. What fun selecting the favours for the cotillion (again the mauve decade), and what a to-do clearing out the dining room and waxing the floor until its surface bore the proper degree of polish. How good natured was Mine Host Chamard, who let us turn his hotel topsy-turvy for the occasion, and what cheers there were when good Miss Chamard,

Mine Host's genial sister, swept across the floor amid deafening applause and took her place at the piano to play a few numbers for us—for in all that vast countryside none there were who could compare with her playing of sprightly waltzes and polkas. It would need a Charles Dickens to describe the gaily whirling couples, the laughter and the gaiety under the soft lamplight. No electricity then—no, sir—nor Charleston nor Black Bottom either. The Boston was the vogue then, we remember.

But Time soon turned the hourglass upside down and our birthdays were laid away, as all birthdays are sooner or later, in old rose and lavender, and the long years have sped by and even the memories of those happy days have grown dim.

So it was that last year when a friend of ours, living abroad in a great manorial estate near Dieppe in Normandy, invited us to her little daughter's birthday fête we accepted with alacrity and crossed from England a day or two earlier than we anticipated to be present on the great day. And great day it was indeed. Worth coming for, from far more many miles than we had come.

The children all made a day of it; they came early in the afternoon and stayed until far into the night. Now a fête in France without fancy cos-

tumes would not be a fête, so all the little guests
came in motley. The little hostess was dressed up
as a cat, and a very lively and vivacious cat she
made, we can assure you. All through the long
summer afternoon they played games—games
strangely similar to the ones our own youngsters
play here in America—in the lovely Old World
garden, and when night fell they sat down to
consume a great birthday cake.

For the evening festivities all the children of
the village as well as their parents had been invited, and how they did enjoy themselves. The
little boys raced about as little boys will anywhere, getting into all sorts of mischief, while
the little girls, more sedate, demurely sought vantage points from which to view the fireworks.
What happy, excited oohs! and aahs! greeted
each pyrotechnic display, and what shrieks of
shrill delight when an unusually elaborate piece
was touched off. It was a happy, tired group of
youngsters that were sent packing homeward
with their pockets and "tummies" bulging with
good things, and none was happier and none more
tired than the little hostess herself, save possibly
her fond mother, who had planned and brought
all this happiness to so many.

Yes, birthdays, save for occasional pleasant exceptions like the above, are things of the past. But meanwhile we give full warning, woe betide the first young person that gets up and offers us his seat in a street car! While politeness is a most desirable attribute and to be highly commended, still it can be overdone, and there is such a thing as justifiable homicide.

"Oh, do let me see our hero!"

Hero Worship

ONE of the most pleasant features of travelling along the great highway called Life is the number of interesting and friendly souls that we meet on that journey. By that we don't mean the "big wigs" and celebrities, but interesting individuals who somehow for one reason or another stand above or apart from their fellow men and who appeal to one's imagination.

For, let us confess it at once, we have no patience with hero worshippers. We have no use for lion hunters, and we can't understand the mentality of those who will stand for hours on a street corner, possibly in a downpour of rain, merely to catch a glimpse of some celebrity as he passes by. We've the utmost contempt for those who cause a near riot trying to crowd into a theatre merely because Mary Pickford or Jack

Barrymore is present in person. This type of
human being drives us wild. We recall one particularly obnoxious example of the species—a
large pulpy-looking personage who was always
in the vanguard when celebrities were around
and whose only claim to fame was the fact, as
he announced loudly and continuously, that he
was "the boy in the brown derby who led the
cheering at the Republican Convention in 1912."

On one occasion, at a semi-public reception
given for the Prince of Wales, we actually felt
keen embarrassment at the conduct of our fellow citizens, who, in their enthusiasm and curio-
sity, well nigh mobbed the young fellow. Not
content with standing and staring at the heir to
the British throne, they even insisted upon crowd-
ing around him while he attempted to dance, so
that his aides had to form a hollow square, in the
centre of which the unfortunate Prince and his
more unfortunate—though she would no doubt
refute the adjective—partner danced. No wonder the Prince was overcome with embarrassment. It was the same with that splendid young
sportsman Lindbergh. We nearly killed him in
our enthusiasm. Not that he didn't deserve adu-
lation; he deserved everything he got and lots
more, but judging from the tired, embarrassed

expression on his face there would have been many happier ways of showing our appreciation than by completely mobbing him.

Our antipathy to hero worship is of long standing. Possibly it may have come from the fact that as a youngster we were once kissed by Admiral Schley, the hero of the Battle of Santiago, and not being French we were not used to the accolade. But more probably our antipathy arises from shyness. When we were introduced to a celebrity we never knew just what to say. We recall once at a dance our hostess was somewhat taken aback when we demurred at being introduced to the lion of the evening, Earl Beatty. It was not that we didn't admire him; on the contrary, we always felt that he was one of the most picturesque and bravest figures of the war. But what had we in common? We couldn't very well ask him how his jolly old fleet was, and what else was there to talk about? So we missed that opportunity. In fact, the only two celebrities we ever felt at home with on meeting them were Feisal, the King of the Hedjaz, who couldn't speak English, and Colonel Lawrence, of Arabian fame, who appeared to be even shyer than we were.

But with other travellers on life's highroad things are different. Not knowing who they are,

one is not overawed by the aura of greatness that
shines about a celebrity. Being gregarious and fond
of our fellow men, we almost always have a
friendly encounter on our travels. We recall once
crossing the English Channel and making friends
with a delightful elderly Englishman. Big, red-
faced, he might easily have posed for the original
John Bull. And he was English to the marrow.
Delightfully so. Far from being offensive, his
enthusiasm for his country was a delight to see,
and the way he quaffed his beer was a sight for
the gods. We were sorry when our roads parted
—and they have never crossed again. One
summer, while viewing Leonardo da Vinci's masterpiece in Milan, we were joined by a young
American farmer from one of the Dakotas. He
had travelled through England, France, and Swit-
zerland for two months on forty dollars, and had
ten dollars and three weeks in which to tour Italy
before his boat sailed for home from Genoa (he
had a return ticket, fortunately). He refused
even the loan of a few dollars, and we last saw
him waving cheerfully from the train window
on his way to Venice. His was the spirit that con-
quers worlds.

Then there were the two jolly girls on a tour
of the New England States in an automobile

truck painted a dazzling blue and labelled "The Bookworm Express." Taking a tip from Christopher Morley's *Parnassus on Wheels,* they had converted a truck into a bookstore and were cheerfully dispensing culture and pleasure to the natives. I suppose next year we'll probably encounter these young ladies operating a flying bookstore in an airplane. For we understand that a flying cigar store is already in operation by one of the great tobacco companies.

Not long since, as we were waiting to be ferried across Long Island Sound, our car suddenly received a terrific jolt that threw it violently into the car ahead. Indignantly we leaped from the car to pour the vials of our wrath upon the head of the miscreants who had bumped into us. But our anger melted away when we beheld an elderly gentleman who looked as if he might have stepped from the pages of Thackeray seated at the wheel of what must have been the original model Franklin car, and smiling benignly at us.

"I'm terribly sorry," he said, "but my left arm is somewhat paralyzed. I can't apply the emergency brake." Beside him sat the sweetest old lady in the world.

What could we say? Except for the shock to our nerves we'd suffered no injury, and the old gentleman's right lamp was stove in and his front tire had gone flat. But that didn't worry him at all. So it was that our wrath melted away and we found ourself changing the front tire for him and actually enjoying it, chatting pleasantly meanwhile with the engaging old couple. The last we saw of Darby and Joan, the former had presented the latter with a copy of Richard Halliburton's *The Royal Road to Romance*.

Now, we ask you, could there have been a more perfect climax?

Fads and Fancies

MAN, it has been remarked—and no doubt will often be remarked again—is a funny animal. He needs diversion. He will spend freely for entertainment money that he would and does grudge for actual necessities. Furthermore, in seeking his entertainment he is possessed of somewhat sheeplike qualities. He will follow blindly where someone else has led. Particularly is this the case of some fad or fancy that happens to catch the public eye. Who could have foretold the craze that swept the country for the crossword puzzle? Here was a form of entertainment certainly not new, for we can remember it in our youth in the puzzle pages of the Sunday editions. Suddenly someone revives it and raises it to the dignity of a book. It hangs fire for a minute, suddenly catches on and sweeps not only the entire country but other nations as well. Publishers fall all over themselves in their efforts to rush new crossword puzzle books off the presses. To-day, the newspapers still carry a daily crossword puzzle and the nth book in the series is selling like hot cakes. No doubt if all the crossword puzzle books sold during the craze were laid end to end they would reach God knows where and probably back.

The earliest puzzle "craze" that we can remember—and we have but the dimmest recollection of it—was a puzzle called "Pigs in Clover." The object was to keep the pigs out of the clover. Just why this proved so popular heaven alone knows, but it was, and the mauve decade outdid itself in a frenzy to buy and solve this knotty problem. Not that there was any money in it—perish the thought. There was merely the smug joy of accomplishment. Much like filling an inside straight or a three-card flush in poker—and there is satisfaction in that, you will admit.

In that era, too, many strange and weird games were popular, though the more serious minded confined their attention to whist and occasionally euchre—bridge, auction and contract, not having emerged from nebulous oblivion yet. We vaguely recall a game called halma, while we were an enthusiastic follower of parchesi and lotto. Anagrams was a very genteel parlour game popular with the grown-ups and said to be a great stimulus for the brain.

Where have all these old favourites gone? Into the limbo of the forgotten, no doubt, together with the magic lantern, the stereopticon, and the kaleidoscope, that fascinating instrument not unlike a telescope, in which one applied one's eye at the end of a cylinder and watched myriad pieces of coloured glass arrange themselves in all manner of lovely combinations at the other end of the cylinder, as it was rotated by hand.

Along about the turn of the century, or later if we recall correctly, ping-pong became all the rage. You all remember how this was played on a table marked like a tennis court, with a celluloid ball and two bats and a net. It had a tremendous vogue for a year or two and no home was complete without a ping-pong set; then it died down and vanished almost completely. Oddly enough, however, the sporting goods dealers and department stores report a revival of interest in the game, and it is just possible that it may be resurrected and restored to public favour.

A craze that was almost universal in America and that came along about this time was somewhat utilitarian in character and certainly blighting in results. This was the craze for making art objects of burnt wood and burnt leather. Talk about burnt offerings! The baneful effects of pyrography, as the gentle art was called, are still with us to-day. The craze spread throughout the land like a plague. Clubs were formed, communities were organized, and all set to work in earnest. From simple pipe racks with a flower design the public spread their efforts to sofa pillows with Gibson Girl heads on them. From pillows they jumped to screens, from screens to tables, until finally no piece of furniture was safe from these firebugs. Eventually the craze died down, due perhaps to the fact that our ideas of interior decoration were changing and, praise be, improving.

For a while the burnt wood craze was followed by a craze for jigsaw puzzles. People not only spent hours piecing jigsaw puzzles together, but many invested in jigsaws themselves and set to work to manufacture them. But the craze was much less violent than the burnt wood mania and was soon laid away, if not in old lace and lavender, at least in sawdust and ashes.

We seemed to slumber along then for several years with no particularly violent craze for amusements. There were a few mild epidemics of one sort or another, but we went the even tenor of our way until one fine morning we awoke to find mah jong in our midst. Someone —again anonymous—browsing in China had found the century-old game of the mandarins and unloaded it on the poor old U. S. A. What a craze that was! People paid all manner of premiums to get a set. Companies sprang up for their importation and even for their manufacture.

And the prices they asked for sets in the early days! Bitten by the bug, we rushed out and purchased one that we could ill afford for $25.50. Only last week we saw an identical set for sale at $1.69! For a little more than a year the boom lasted; then it collapsed utterly and completely.

Phoenix-like from the ashes of the mah jong craze the crossword puzzle poked its ugly (we are a little bitter, as you can see) head and was welcomed to the bosom of the nation. Celebrities not only solved puzzles but created them, and there were actual crossword tournaments. The number of happy homes that were broken up by this curse was innumerable. Babies wailed unattended, countless kettles boiled over unheeded, and the home went to rack and ruin while Mother worked out the daily crossword puzzle. No one was safe from it. Old and young, men and women did them. They had no shame, and they solved them everywhere—on trains, and in the theatre, even at the opera. Yes, the crossword puzzle bug was one of the most violent that ever attacked the genus *homo sapiens*.

What will take its place? Gentle reader, if we knew we'd not be writing this. We'd be in the counting room counting our ill-gotten gains.

Shakespeare it was who said that

> There is a tide in the affairs of men
> Which taken at the flood, leads on to fortune.

The tide is there waiting. In which direction will it flow? Your guess is as good as ours. Go to it.

"who's been tearing up my 400-year-old atlas!?!"

"I simply had to have the latest thing in doilies for my tea yesterday, hadn't I? do be sensible."

Our Own Five-Foot Shelf

AT a certain time of year when the nights
are growing cool and the days appreciably
shorter, someone invariably writes to the
papers an open letter suggesting a list of the books
one should have with him in the event of being
cast away on a desert isle for the rest of his life.
Just who originated this idea is lost in the mists
of time, but we suspect that early reading of *The
Swiss Family Robinson* had something to do with
it. Anyway, it is a fascinating game whether or
not your horoscope contains a shipwreck.

Now, frankly, we don't ever expect to be ship-
wrecked—much less cast away on a desert isle
with a packet of books for company. But we do
like to pause every now and then and turn over
in our mind our favourite books: those volumes
that have been with us these many long years and
which we take pleasure in reading over and over
again. Why, there are some books we really believe we have read dozens of times, and some, like

Pickwick Papers—or rather parts of it—we read almost yearly.

Our list is not a very long one, but it is varied, for if we were to start on a journey toward eternity or on any other long tedious trip, we should like variety. So it is that our list includes all manner of writing and our humble library contains a fairly represenative list of titles.

The trouble, it seems to us, with "Vox Populi," "Paterfamilias," and other celebrated anonymities, who write and give long lists of books suitable for castaways or hermits, is that they incline to take a very gloomy and depressing view of things. Life is earnest, life's sincere. They begin always by heading their lists with the Bible, which is as it should be. But then they complete their lists with most of Shakespeare, some Herodotus, perhaps a little Plutarch, and by way of diversion a little Horace. Undoubtedly here is meat for soul and body. Good solid vitamines. But Plutarch and even Shakespeare as a steady diet would pall. So it is that our list undoubtedly would not please the scholarly. Yet all the books on it are old friends, tried and true.

To begin with, let's put down *Vanity Fair*. Almost any other volume of Thackeray would do, but *Vanity Fair* is just a little our favourite.

As a mater of fact, Dickens might just as well head the list, for *Pickwick Papers* is the most thoroughly entertaining reading we've yet discovered, though *Oliver Twist* and *A Tale of Two Cities* are favourites too. But if we are to confine our precious five-foot shelf to one volume of an author, then *Vanity Fair* and *Pickwick Papers* it shall be. Oddly enough, *Pickwick Papers* was the first actual book we ever possessed, excepting of course *Mother Goose* and other children's books. In fact, we were given it at such an early age that it was some years before we could make head or tail of it. So much for Dickens. Skipping a bit, we come to Kipling. Here again is a hard choice. Shall we pass up *Kim* and *Captains Courageous?* Yes, hard as it is, we must, for, for sheer joy and pleasure, refer us to *The Brushwood Boy.* The lovely illusive imagery of that tale of Kipling's has never been surpassed, and we would not want to be without it.

Then we'd include in the same vein Kenneth Graham's *Wind in the Willows.* But this is a child's book, you may demur. Granted, but unfortunately we are still enough of a child to read and reread the tale with the keenest enjoyment. Possibly it is this same childishness that has made us read, at least five times, Christopher Morley's

Thunder on the Left. So we must be sure to take along this important volume. Then we would not be without John Galsworthy's masterpiece, *The Foryte Saga.* Here is interest enough to stave off ennui for years.

So far we've included mostly imaginative fiction. For an antidote and because we believe it a really great book, we'd take Sinclair Lewis's *Babbitt* with us, and if that is not enough realism, we should also include—and this will surprise you —Theodore Dreiser's *An American Tragedy.* Powerful studies these two, and well worth reading. In direct contrast we would not want to be without Louis Hémon's epic of the simple French-Canadian peasant *Maria Chapdelaine*—a truly wonderful example of finished prose.

When it comes to adventure, there is one volume—and we've read hundreds of excellent ones —that stands in a class by itself, we feel. That is Sir Ernest Shackleton's marvellous epic *South.* Where can one find greater thrills or greater heroism than in the story of Shackleton's attempt on the South Pole or his fight for life in an open boat on the Wedell Sea? Even *Moby Dick* pales in comparison.

For history we'd probably include a volume of Parkman's *History of Canada*—his pages are so full of colourful reading—though no doubt many would incline to Wells's *Outline of History* as being broader in scope. If we include a volume of biography—and we certainly should—we've had more enjoyment from Lytton Strachey's *Queen Victoria* than from almost any other biography.

In lighter vein, if we felt it was needed—and we doubt this, as humour on a desert isle might seem a trifle forced—we'd take along a volume of Stephen Leacock's *Nonsense Novels* or Donald Ogden Stewart's *Parody Outline of History,* the only book of humour, except *Alice in Wonderland,* that we can recall having read and laughed over more than once.

On looking over our list we hardly feel that we could be cast away without Robert Louis Stevenson's *Treasure Island,* and if there were room we should include a volume of Dumas as well as one of Victor Hugo. And O. Henry's *Four Million* and Poe's *Tales* would certainly vary the monotony considerably. *Bob, Son of Battle,* Ollivant's famous dog story, grows more fascinating, too, with constant reading.

Finally, there is another volume, perhaps not as well known as it deserves to be, that gives us infinite pleasure each time we read it, and that is

The Further Side of Silence. (There's a real title for you, full of mystery of the Malayan jungles in itself.) These tales of the Malay Peninsula by Sir Hugh Clifford, former Governor of the Malay States, are perhaps the most fascinating folk stories that we have ever encountered, and although we almost know them by heart we've put them down for a rereading in the not-too-distant future.

We might run our list on into infinity. We know it is sadly lacking in many respects and a poor piece of selection. Yet it is a sincere list. Each item on it has contributed much pleasure to the passing of the years. And in the pages of the volumes we feel at home. The coming years will add to the list, will bring new favourites. But we feel sure they will not displace the old ones—they have been too long and too deeply embedded in the cockles of our heart.

"this is the life!"

"feefteen cents
I dive!"

Wanderlust

WITH all their skill and years of experience there are two afflictions that beset the human race for which the doctors—learned men, mark ye, Antonio—have never been able to find a cure: homesickness and the wanderlust. But are these two real afflictions? Are they not, perhaps, blessings in disguise? The one drawing us into a closer spiritual kinship with our dear ones, and the other opening new joys and delights to the eyes. Anyway, homesickness is easily disposed of. It comes early, but once the attack is over you are not, except in rare cases, apt to suffer its pangs again. To be sure, it's grievous while it lasts and time is the only remedy, but it has one advantage—it inoculates its victim against itself.

The wanderlust is a horse of a different colour. It's much less painful. At times it is almost pleasant. It, like love, they tell me, brings a sweet nostalgia with it. But it, unlike homesickness, recurs again and again, sometimes more virulent, again in milder form. You never can tell just when it's going to strike you. The spring is a favourite time. It seems to ride in on the wave of spring fever that is so prevalent. But the wanderlust is by no means confined to the spring. You can get it in the dead of winter; you can get it any time, anywhere. It is just as catching in age as it is in youth. I've known it to strike old ladies of ninety, and off they've started on a journey to the Holy Land; and I've seen youths throw up a perfectly good career at its beck and call.

Once you've got the wanderlust you're helpless in its toils—that is, at least, until the creature's desire is satisfied or time has worn its fangs down to innocuousness.

A vacation is not a real vacation, it seems to me, that does not give one complete relaxation or change. Two sorts fill the bill admirably; one, a trip off into the woods where one gets close to nature, and the other, a trip to foreign shores.

What a pleasure, apart from the history of a country, or its architecture or its scenic beauty, it is to study the people themselves. To form one's own conclusion of the various races. It would be difficult to name one's favourite country, for personally, in a recent tour of the Continent I found all of them so charming that it was difficult to decide. I never failed to meet with anything but the utmost consideration everywhere. I think, however, that the English are the most polite and considerate, and I've yet to find a striking example of the much touted British aloofness. During the war the British outdid themselves for the "Yanks." I even had an officer give up his bed one night in 1918 in London so that I might not have to sit up all night. The same seems to hold true after the war. The conductors on the buses, the porters at the railway stations—even the taxi drivers—are genuinely polite, and of course when it comes to manners no one quite comes up to the London "bobby."

On the trains, on my journey, far from being aloof, the average Britisher was only too keen to engage you in conversation. One incident I recall in particular. Coming up on the boat from Southampton to London the compartment was filled with Britishers except for an old gentleman and his flapper daughter and myself. The daughter, a nice young thing with the breezy assurance of American youth, oblivious to the nationality of

our fellow travellers, was regaling the compartment with her views of England and the English.
It was her first trip over, and her views of things
British were certainly frank and to say the least
uncomplimentary, especially when comparing
them with things American. Did the Britishers
object? On the contrary, they enjoyed the com-
ments on themselves immensely and kept urging
her on to new heights (or depths) and ended by
planning a complete schedule for each day of her
stay so that she should not miss any important
sight. Yet the unthinking American will say that
the Englishman is cold and has no sense of
humour!

I confess I love the French. They have such
esprit, such *joie de vivre,* and they make life so
vital and interesting. To be sure, they have traits
that can't be admired, but no doubt they have
far fewer of these than we as a nation have. The
very first thing they did to me on landing in
France when last I visited them was to put me
under arrest for bringing in a package of a hundred cigarettes, which I carried in my pocket and
had forgotten to declare. Was it a serious and solemn occasion? Anything but. Of course, for the
first few moments there were wild gesticulations
and a vivid flow of oratory. But nothing dis-

agreeable, and after the exchange of some pleas-
antries—in bad French on my part—the customs
officer with the grace of a Chesterfield (no pun
intended) announced that while he regretted it
extremely he would have to fine me 150 francs
(about $2.50 at the time), and handed me back
the cigarettes. Not so bad when you consider that
a friend on the same channel steamer who had
declared his cigarettes was charged precisely the
same amount as duty.

As for the Italians, from being a skeptic who
since childhood days looked upon the entire nation as "wops," I've come to consider them a great
race. Of all the countries Italy has changed the
most for the better since the war. For the Italians
seem to have once more come into their own—
to have caught something of the spirit of the
Cæsars, and to have taken their place in the sun
as one of the great nations of the world. Whether
you believe in Mussolini's rule or not—and it
doesn't make much difference whether you do
or not—Italy owes him a tremendous debt. To
spend months in Italy and never see a beggar
—and this is true even of Naples; to wander
through the country and see prosperity on all
sides and a contented, happy people, prosperous
and busy where before poverty and idleness

walked hand in hand, is to make you pause and ponder. To have one's baggage unlocked and not tampered with and then even to roam through the back alleys of Venice long after midnight unarmed and unmolested is an experience new to the American in Italy. Yet it is being done as this is being written. And for this the Italian has only himself to thank, himself and Mussolini. And everywhere the same unfailing courtesy, from conductors on the railroads to cabin boys on the Italian liners.

And what is true of England, France, and Italy is no doubt true of other countries, and some day when the wanderlust strikes again—and already the preliminary symptoms are beginning to make themselves felt—I'll hie me to other pastures new, and lo! there'll be copy enough for another book.

Moonlight and Magic

THE old alchemists, it has always seemed to us, wasted a lot of time trying to find a means of transmuting the base metals into gold. They were always doddering about trying one experiment after another, wasting away lifetimes and often blowing themselves up in their futile efforts to find the elusive solution.

And all the time the miracle was being performed daily, or rather nightly, about them. Right before their eyes nature performed the feat for which they sought eagerly and they were too blind to see it.

For moonlight turns dross into pure gold if anything ever did, you'll readily agree. Nothing, even the ugliest and dreariest, but assumes new shapes and new forms under the magic of moonlight. Old familiar objects that you've seen every day of your life and never noticed twice because of their being so commonplace, assume a dignity and a mystery that make them seem fantastic and unreal.

And as it changes inanimate objects, the moon seems to exert a powerful influence on the animate. The animal kingdom is sensibly affected by it, and its influence on man and his destiny is too well known to comment upon. Cases of moonstroke in mediæval days were as numerous as cases of sunstroke nowadays, and Shakespeare is full of references to moon madness. While this theory of lunar insanity is discredited to-day, still there are few, I'll venture to say, who'd care to sleep with the rays of the moon falling upon them.

Now we recognize Her Majesty the Moon as a beneficent goddess. As an aid to Cupid she has no peer, for moonlight makes us all a little sentimental, and it is a fairly hardened nature that does not come under the witchery of her rays.

Somewhat sentimental by nature, a full moon affects us deeply. It fills us—and we suppose this is common to all mankind—with a sweet melancholy, accompanied, however, by great peace of mind. Under its rays we fall into deep reveries. We dream great dreams; the trivial, petty business of living slips from our shoulders like a mantle abandoned.

Unconsciously our mind reverts to the past— the great days of the ages pass in review before us. A new humbleness envelops us. We are conscious of the infinitesimal rôle we play in the cosmos. Then, ambition stirring, we make all sorts of brave resolutions for the future and yet all the while a sweet melancholy pervades, and we despair of the futility of mankind.

We have fond memories of moonlight nights, memories etched deeply upon our consciousness. We recall clear winter nights in the Far North where the moon cast her beams over a silent world and the cold was so intense that the breath froze on one's lips. On such nights as these we used to wander to the top of a near-by hill and gaze at the sleeping world at our feet. All around us the mountains raised lofty snow-clad summits against a cloudless sky. Below us lay the sombre pine-clad forests with the lordly Saguenay River, a broad black sinister ribbon, winding its way through the snow and ice to the St. Lawrence. And all the while the aurora borealis flung its fantastic beams in a canopy of glory over our head. Hours we'd spend in contemplation until the cold drove us within.

Nights such as this are difficult to forget. Nor can we forget summer nights, paddling along

quietly in a canoe on wilderness lakes, far from
the haunts of man, with the moon making a broad
beam of silver on the water up which we slowly
paddled, while the only sounds that broke the
stillness were the mournful cries of the owl from
the depths of the forest.

And the beauty of Paris by moonlight! If ever
the lily were painted, it is when a full moon rises
over the lovely old city. Walk along the banks of
the Seine. Was there ever such a sight! The pont
Alexandre III is a gossamer fairy thing, and even
the solid bulk of Notre Dame takes on new and
unearthly splendour.

And when you've done with Paris, come with
me to Rome. Climb one of the seven hills of this
city on a night when Luna is in full splendour.
What a sight for mere mortals! All around you,
spread in jewelled splendour, lies the Eternal City.
In the distance St. Peter's raises its lofty dome
over the surrounding houses. The cypresses of the
Borghese Gardens make a dark note in the golden
picture. Faintly you can discern the Coliseum
and Hadrian's Tomb, and all the while, the Tiber
flows on, a sheet of silver through the glory that
is Rome.

But of all the sights we recall, and they have
been many, the most perfect was a night of full

Moonlight and Magic

moon in Venice. Our gondola shot us through the molten silver of the Grand Canal to the Giudecca whereon was moored a large flat-decked barge. Gaily trapped out in bright lanterns, the deck of the barge had been cleared for dancing, and guests sat at small tables while an orchestra played soft airs.

About midnight, when the moon was most nearly perfect, the lanterns and all the lights on the barge were extinguished. The orchestra began softly playing an old and lovely waltz of Strauss. Mechanically almost, as if bewitched, the couples moved gracefully over the floor in the moonlight, and as they danced, the barge moved slowly up the Giudecca Canal, propelled by some unseen force. That for us was the hour of hours. Never shall we forget it, never shall we relive it. The image of the scene, the soft music, the balmy air, the moon on the old palazzos as we moved slowly by them, those are things that time, adversity, or other evils can never, never obliterate.

Do you wonder, then, that we are a humble votary of Diana?

The Great American Pastime

WHY is it, we wonder, that travel makes a snob of us? Ordinarily, we are really very democratic and gregarious, and like the company of our fellow men. In fact, we have a strong penchant for making friends with the proletariat, preferring to smoke a friendly pipe with the superintendent of our neighbour's vast estate or to chat awhile with our friend the rural philosopher who disguises himself as a clerk, in a linen duster, in the crossroads general store of our little country town rather than engage in formal after-dinner conversations.

But when we travel we draw ourselves into a shell, as it were, and seeking a secluded corner of the observation car, view in solitary aloofness the unfolding scenery, although at the same time we must admit watching out of the corner of our eye our fellow travellers.

No doubt this "snobbishness," if we wish to

call it this (we should prefer rather this "inhibition"—that sounds more pleasing somehow), is peculiar to us, for we haven't noticed that travelling affects others much in this manner. On the contrary, travelling seems to make most mortals extremely garrulous, and they prattle away at high speed, paying much more attention to a recital of Cousin Katie's latest ailments than to the unfolding glories of nature.

Now, travelling has always been to us the keenest delight. The mere thought of a trip throws us into a paroxysm of anticipation truly delightful. It doesn't matter much where we are going; we are content just to be on a boat or a train going somewhere. We even get a mild sort of thrill crossing on a ferry from Oakland to San Francisco. Why, a twenty-minute sail up New York Harbour from Staten Island to the Battery is sheer joy as we watch the panorama of Manhattan unfold before our eyes.

It is a funny thing how people's real nature comes to the surface in travelling, just as it does in a camping trip. One gets to recognize and look for certain types. There is always the woman who wears a cap fastened firmly on her head by yards and yards of veiling that blows hither and yon in everyone's face. She is generally accompanied by

her "better" half—the better you will note is
quoted: an amiable small-mannish man invariably dressed in gray with a gray silk cap pulled
well over his eyes and an inevitable toothpick or
fragment of cigar clutched firmly (likewise
noisily and moistly) in his mouth. Of course he
wears some sort of fraternal emblem dangling
from his watch chain or proudly flaunted on the
lapel of this coat. The women wear smoked
glasses. Furthermore, they may or may not—it
depends whether luck is with you or not—be accompanied by a small boy or girl or both. These
latter, by rising at the crack of dawn, manage
to secure the best seat on the observation platform, which seat they maintain by right of pos-
session and in relays from dawn to dusk, and no
matter how much you may manœuvre you'll
never get that seat away from them.

For the most part they are friendly folk, eager
to exchange views and to tell you their personal
history. Generally they find willing victims, and
the trip is enlivened by personal details of a most
intimate nature. At sea, by feigning seasickness
one may avoid them, but on a train it is well-
nigh impossible. And there is nothing more annoy-
ing than to have the thread of an exciting book
broken into by a tireless dialogue in the adjoining

chair. To be sure one can—that is, if one is fortunate in one's sex—seek the seclusion of the smoking
room, but it's a ten to one chance that it is already
occupied by a breezy individual who greets you
as "brother," though certainly he is no relation,
and who slaps you heartily on the knee and insists
upon telling you the latest one about the Honey-
moon Couple.

One of the strangest phenomena is the woman
who waits eagerly for hours to get a seat on the
observation platform, and when at last she
achieves it, turns her back to the view and
promptly goes to sleep, entirely unperturbed by
the fact that the view is gorgeous or by the angry
glances of a score or so of persons waiting anxiously to gain a foothold on the precious space.
We witnessed this phenomenon in a particularly
extraordinary way. Our train—the Canadian
Pacific's crack transcontinental, the Trans-Can-

ada—was about to take the world-famed drop a thousand feet or more down the side of the mountain into Kicking Horse Canyon. Far below us the track wound in serpentine curves down to roaring Kicking Horse River. The windows of the car were lined with faces. It was a tense moment in a magnificent setting of natural grandeur; and yet opposite us two women sat with their backs to the valley beneath and actually shut their eyes and slept as we plunged downward. Moral turpitude would seem a mild offense compared with this!

But when all is said and done the very worst pest of all is the spoiled small boy. He, we are inclined to think, is largely responsible for our state of aloofness when we travel. Too many trips has he spoiled for us ever to forgive him and to excuse his behaviour on the grounds of youthful exuberance or animal spirits. One brat we remember in particular, for the event is still fresh in our memory.

We set out by rail for a midwinter trip to Florida. We had hardly emerged from the tunnel that connects New York with Jersey when he was at the door inquiring our destination, our ages, our views, etc., incidentally telling us the most intimate details of his own and his parents' lives. Despite the chilliness of his reception and the enforced rudeness of eventually slamming the door in his face, he chose to regard us as kindred spirits and invariably greeted us noisily and sought to engage us in conversation when we appeared on the observation platform—though he never relinquished his hold for a moment on the camp stool upon which he was seated. Our appearance in the diner was always the signal for the withdrawing of the spoon from his mouth—where it reposed most of the time—and the frantic waving of it in the air to announce to his parents and to the car in general our arrival. For three days and three nights we suffered in silence, so it was with a sigh of relief that we disembarked at Miami and went our separate ways.

But alas, we counted our good fortune too soon! For next day as we set out upon a tour of the city in one of those comfortably upholstered behemoths called sightseeing buses, who should we find in the seat next to us but our fiend (we purposely left out the "r" in the word). It took strong will power on our part, when at the alligator farms candidates were sought among the onlookers for the privilege of riding an alligator, not to suggest little Egbert.

Yes, travelling does bring out the best and the

worst in one's character. But nothing, to our way of thinking, is more pleasurable. Already we are hauling steamer trunks out of the attic. Our passage is engaged, and we'll soon start off for a little jaunt. Perhaps this love for travel.is natural, in our case. Our forebears were great voyagers. In fact the best piece of advice our progenitor ever gave us was this: "Beg if you must," he said, "borrow if you have to, even steal if necessary, only be sure to travel." So perhaps we are to be excused if we strive to follow this most excellent advice.

Sightseeing at Home

ONE of the most interesting phases of human nature, to our way of thinking, is that which prompts people living in the midst of interesting and historical places to take no interest in them. It's a standing joke how few New Yorkers have been to the top of the Woolworth Building. Even fewer have taken the trouble to visit the Statue of Liberty. Why, there are even one or two who have never seen *Abie's Irish Rose,* we're told. This lack of appreciation we confess is one of our own failings. In all our life, spent mostly in the heart of New York, we visited the top of the Woolworth Tower only recently for the first time to show the view to an out-of-town friend.

We've found the sightseeing buses the quickest and easiest way to acquire knowledge of a place, and one can always return the next day and visit the spots that require further study. The buses have their drawbacks—there is always at least one loquacious occupant who discourses loudly and at length on any subject that occurs to him or her, though it is generally a garrulous old gentleman. But the worst feature is the attempted humour of the average guide, who mistakenly seems to feel that facetiousness, so called, is part of his stock in trade. In this he is equalled only by the average radio announcer.

But the buses are quick and comfortable, and they are valuable in reaching places away from the city limits, like the Magnolia Gardens in Charleston.

Oddly enough, for some unknown reason— probably the same that prevented our seeing Napoleon's Tomb in Paris—we had never paid a visit to Mount Vernon, though we'd often been a visitor in Washington. Frankly, it was inexcusable on our part. If there is one spot that should be, and is, sacred to an American, it is George Washington's home on the Potomac. However, we've remedied all that now and made a special trip for the very purpose of visiting the spot.

It was like going to an old friend's house, we were so familiar with the estate from reading Paul Wilstach's *Mount Vernon* and many articles

on the same subject. Everything was as we had
expected it to be, only lovelier, with the mansion
set in the midst of its broad lawns and surrounded
by leafy trees in all the glory of their fall foliage,
and in the background the silvery Potomac winding its leisurely way. We could have sat on the
front porch and dreamed for hours of Washington, and the days when the nation was created.
We wished, too, that we might have seen Mount
Vernon alone. It should be studied quietly and
earnestly. The early morning, when the estate
is first opened, would seem the ideal time to visit
the spot. As it was, when we were there the halls
and staircase were crowded and the lawns overrun with schoolgirls and the usual smart alecks,
making "wisecracks" about "Little Old George"
and failing to remove their hats in the house until
warned to do so by an attendant.

Somehow, we felt that the great man would
have resented such an intrusion, and we felt almost glad that he was not there to see it all, even
though the throng had come, many of them from
afar, to honour his memory.

We confess to a feeling of disappointment in
the interior of Mount Vernon. We had not realized that the mansion was so cut up into small
rooms. No doubt this was an economic necessity

to conserve heat, but from the outside of the house we imagined more stately rooms. The Father of His Country would feel at home in modern apartments were it a question of the size of the rooms alone. The bedrooms seemed somewhat dark and dingy, particularly the one the faithful Martha occupied after her distinguished husband's death. The furniture, too, for the most part, was undistinguished, much of it not Washington's. It is, of course, understandable that the custodians have not been able to buy or even find much of the furniture, but we were told that the present owners of Washington's dining table have put such a prohibitive price on it as to render its purchase impossible. If this be true, and we can scarcely credit it, there would seem to be no excuse for such an attitude.

This brings up another similar subject. In the lodge room of the Lodge of Alexandria, of which Washington was the Worshipful Master, there is a case containing relics of him, whose place, it seems to us, is more rightly at Mount Vernon. It is quite fitting and proper that the Lodge should possess and treasure such relics as Washington's Masonic apron, the chair he occupied as Grand Master, the gavel he wielded—all these and any other Masonic relics should be the property of the Lodge, but we don't think that the Lodge should retain the gloves in which he was married, the cups with which the doctor bled him on his deathbed, his pruning knife, and many other relics of his home life. Mount Vernon is the logical and only repository for such Washingtonia. A just and patriotic order such as the Masons should set an example by restoring the relics to the custodians of Mount Vernon. In that way only can we have a truly national shrine.

A word more—the custodians of the estate should be most highly commended for their excellent care of the place. The nation can never be grateful enough to that band of women that rescued the mansion from neglect and decay and is to-day maintaining it in a manner worthy of so noble an object. Particularly were we pleased that the gardens of Mount Vernon were not desecrated by rows of booths of souvenir merchants and hot-dog stands. So far as is humanly possible, these blights have been eliminated.

"Officer, I desire to see some of the sights of your fair city."

"Have you looked in a mirror?"

Discovering a New World

LATELY we've noticed an alarming symptom, a phenomenon almost. We have discovered incipient signs in ourself of becoming a yachtsman. Not that we've inherited a vast fortune sufficient to enable us to travel about in a floating palace, all white and shining with brass. Nothing so fancy as that. But after years of being a confirmed landlubber we've suddenly found ourself becoming very fond of the water and taking the utmost interest in things nautical.

Brought up far from the sea, amid the mountains, our taste ran to land sports, and our most daring nautical experiences were long canoe trips on mountain lakes, with an occasional voyage to Europe—neither one to be recommended as a training school for a nautical education. How the change came about we scarcely know ourself.

It may have been the effect of a very pleasant trip to New London to the Yale-Harvard boat race—and there is no lovelier sight than that of all the pleasure craft concentrated in the Thames River in Connecticut once a year for the annual regatta—or it may have been the six-metre races. For we defy anyone not to get a thrill of pleasure and excitement out of the sight of the graceful yachts on Long Island Sound with the attendant swarm of motor-driven craft. Possibly the Gold Cup Races, with their spills and hair-raising upsets, stirred our sluggish blood. Or it may just have been the nautical convictions of our friends and the tales of sport they told that roused us. Suffice to say something stirred within us and we woke to discover a new world.

Our real conversion, however, that threatens to be permanent—occurred but a short while ago. We were in a party that visited Savannah, Ga. In the party were several motorboat enthusiasts, among them was a blonde-haired, blue-eyed girl of some twenty years of age. With her healthy tan and delicate colouring she looked as if she'd stepped down from the prow of some old viking ship. But she wasn't interested in viking ships, not she! Her interest was centred on a strange species of craft with a motor that one hung over the stern as one would crook an umbrella over one's arm—and how she could make those frail eggshells travel along! For she was Helen Hentschell fresh from her triumph in breaking the world's speed record for these craft at Detroit.

There must have been fifty of these outboard motorboats on hand at Savannah, and they skipped and jumped about all day long like so many animated waterbugs. We watched them for hours at a stretch, fascinated no less by their names than by their antics. There was the *Baby Whale,* the *Cutie Craft,* and the *Boy Friend,* the *Cavalier, Nut'n Much,* the *Scat,* the *Sneeze Twice,* and countless others. Finally, one of the pilots must have seen the wistful look in our eyes, for he stopped his craft—the *Boy Friend* it was—and motioned us aboard.

Now, we've been up in an airplane, driven a motorcycle, even jumped on skis, but this new sport out-thrilled them all. With only a quarter of an inch between us and the water, the *Boy Friend* leaped from the top of one wave to another and spanked them soundly as she passed over them. Sheets of water flew in our face as we raced along; we clung on like grim death as we skittered around corners, we passed directly under the overhanging stern of a yacht and bounced like a rubber ball when we hit the wake of a passing motorboat. Finally, after a few resounding spanks that left us black and blue, we drew up alongside the dock breathless but happy, and a convert to these delightful craft.

In fact, so enthusiastic did we become that next day, encouraged perhaps by a mint julep or two, which only Southerners can make, we had an idea. We proposed a grand Novice International Outboard Motor Race for all comers who had never driven the craft before. The list was made up. His Honour, Dr. Ernest Poulin, one time acting mayor of Montreal, would represent Canada; Orton Tewson, the distinguished literary critic (after a little urging, and mildly protesting), would fly the British flag; while General Leslie Kincaid, our host, and ourself would defend the United States. Helen Hentschell lent us her life preserver, which we hastily buckled on. Someone thrust a yachting cap on His Honour the Mayor's head, but the General was the first away in the jaunty *Cavalier*. Alas, he was the only one to get away! The Mayor got held up by amiably posing for the press photographers, and the rest of us were waved off the course by annoyed officials who were trying to establish a new world's record. So the General won the race and the glory. And glory it was, too, for he sped by at an amazing clip. The only trouble was that no one had instructed him how to stop the boat. Grimly he faced the prospect of dashing about on the water till his gasoline gave out. Fortunately, or unfortunately, his engine died, and he leaped from Scylla to Charybdis, for he couldn't start it again to get to the dock. We had our last view of the General working desperately and vainly to turn the motor over before the outgoing tide carried him off into the thickening gloom of the night.

But the work had been done, the seed sown. We'd become a fan, and sometime, if by chance you are in our neighbourhood and hear a noise like a series of explosions, don't wonder. It's not a still. It's merely us trying out the *Allouette*, for even though we've not bought it yet, we've already named the craft in honour of a certain pleasant evening spent with our genial and vocal friend, the acting Mayor of ye ancient city of Montreal.

The Open Season for Art

WE HOLD no brief for winter. Time was when we enjoyed the snow and ice. We can even remember jumping purposely into a snowdrift and rolling about for the sheer pleasure of it, until we were wringing wet and so cold that our hands and feet were numb. That was long, long ago. To-day even the thought of such a thing sends shivers down our back, and the annual approach of winter fills us with a dread that is scarce dispelled by plans—sometimes realized, more often not—for sojourns in more fortunate climes where Jack Frost never ventures.

Winter in the city to us is particularly obnoxious. For snow substitute dirty slush, and for clear bracing air substitute freezing draughts, and you have it. But winter in the city has one consolation—it brings the art exhibits; and we must frankly confess to a fondness for paintings and sculpture. Unfortunately the exchequer forbids our being a collector. Perhaps this is just as well, for our taste is purely personal, and when it comes to art we are what might be called self-made. What little knowledge we have has been gleaned from friendly artists, long days spent in the museums, informal chats with our friends the art dealers, and many happy and entertaining hours spent in the studios of our artist friends. For the artists are friendly folk. Theirs is a kindly philosophy. They take a particularly tolerant view of life which in these days of poking one's nose into the other fellow's business is most refreshing.

So it is that we are glad when winter comes and we can witness the result of their summer labours—the fruit of long days by the sea, or in the mountains, or in those spots where beauty eludes all but true artists' eyes.

Now we have the utmost interest in the old masters. Their work is eternal and their canvases unrivalled. Their masterpieces, like the great works of the architect, can never be forgotten. They indeed are supreme for all time. None the less, we have a great liking, a partiality almost, for modern art. Don't misunderstand us. By "modern" we do not mean the cubists or the

futurists or those Russian gentlemen who have
taken to making pictures out of bits of wood, or
metal, or cotton, or God knows what. To us
their canvases are meaningless. Undoubtedly they
are of some use in that they are trying to express
an idea, and no doubt they represent progress,
but progress is nearly always ugly and disagree-
able. No, by modern we mean the artists at work
to-day or who lived in recent years. Their work
seems so alive, so full of expression that it gives
great promise for the future. Take some of the
great ones—Sargent, Augustus John, Orpen,
Zuloaga, László, Matisse, Picasso, etc.—here are
names to conjure with. And the sculptors—
Rodin, Davidson, Manship, Borglum, Epstein,
MacMonnies, Partridge, etc.—surely they reach
new heights with the chisel.

And there are hosts of younger men doing great
things to-day, whose work it is a pleasure to see.
Visit the Royal Academy Exhibit in London, the
salons in Paris, the great International Exhibit
at the Carnegie Institute in Pittsburgh, or the
Spring and Fall Academy Exhibitions in New
York. We'll wager there are pleasures galore for
anyone with the slightest sense of the beautiful.
Nor is talent confined to the larger exhibitions.
Almost any week in winter finds the art dealers

of our large cities holding exhibits of contemporary art.

We get a great deal of fun out of these exhibits, and we've learned to look forward to them with much pleasure.

There are two shows that can be classed as unusual in every sense of the word, out of which we get much quiet enjoyment each year. The first of these is the annual exhibit of the New Society of Painters and Sculptors, and the other the Independents' Exhibition held each winter in New York. For these are the ultra moderns. At the New Society only members of the society may exhibit, but the Independents' show is a free for all. That is to say, a hanging fee is necessary, but there are no prizes and no jury, and anyone may exhibit. Here is a veritable museum of "modern" art. Futurism, cubism, and all the other "isms" run riot here, and there is a strong undercurrent of what for want of a better term might be labelled "art calendar" art. A truly amazing collection generally. Just where most of the exhibitors obtain their knowledge of painting, and particularly of anatomy, would be interesting to know. Offhand, from the mushroom, sofa-pillow-like qualities of their figures, we might guess somewhere in Turkey. And judging from the violent colour combinations the spectrum is an unknown quantity with them. Anyway, when it comes to nudes—even though geometrically wrong—they have the merit of frankness, and it is quite evident that most of the artists never have been subsidized by the well-known manufacturer, Mr. Gillette.

Next to the *Salon des Humoristes* in Paris there is no art exhibition more entertaining—mind you, not instructive—than this. And that reminds us, why shouldn't we have an annual Humorists' Salon in America? Or do the authorities believe the Independent Show supplies this want? We wonder.

Some Obsolete Laws

BEFORE we begin, in order not to mislead anyone, this is not to be an anti-prohibition treatise. We may have our opinions as to the Volstead Act, its enforcement, its use, and its efficiency, but we have no intention of voicing them here. No, we've another axe to grind, another law to rail against, and that is our automobile speed laws. Right away let us hasten to explain we've never been arrested or fined for speeding. (We pause to knock on wood.) Once in a while, engaged in an absorbing conversation with a friend, we have dashed through a crossing in defiance of a red light set against us and have received a just and extremely thorough reprimand from the officer on duty. One time we were waved angrily to the side of the road by an irate officer who claimed that we were going more than twenty-five miles an hour within the limits of a township. Possibly we were, but there were no houses anywhere around and no traffic, and we honestly thought we were in the open country. Our sincerity apparently impressed the officer, for he shut the summons book resignedly and waved to us to be on our way, which we lost no time in being, humbly and gratefully.

No, our quarrel with the speed laws is not a personal one, nor has it anything to do with the officers who enforce them—for the most part they do their duty faithfully and well. Our contention is that speed laws are antiquated and entirely unnecessary. We've taken motor trips in Europe wherein we had many an opportunity to study motoring on the Continent, where speed laws are, to say the least, scarcely noticeable and certainly in no way objectionable.

And if they are not needed in Europe they certainly are not a whit more necessary to us, for the average American is generally a first-class driver. If one uses judgment and common sense in driving there is no reason why he shouldn't be permitted to drive just as fast as conditions allow him. If there is an open country road ahead, why shouldn't one go forty or fifty miles an hour if one cares to? What more exasperating to an able-minded man driving his own car than to feel that a motorcycle policeman may appear at any minute or pop out from behind the next bush only too happy to hand the offending driver a "ticket"? And what better cause of heart failure can you imagine than the put-put of the motor-cycle as it catches up with you and you realize that you are in for a summons and untold incon-venience and annoyance? It is all so unnecessary. Modern mechanism has evolved brakes of such quick action that the machine travelling at a good rate of speed can be checked very easily, and the good driver never takes chances. It is the reckless driver, the fool in the car, who takes chances, who disregards or is ignorant of the traffic laws, and who jeopardizes the lives of others by his recklessness and carelessness, that we want to see locked up or at least fined and cleared off the road until he learns to behave himself. He is the real culprit, not the steady driver who puts on a burst of speed when conditions warrant it. For few people are killed by speeding, as some states are coming to realize.

Nor do we advocate the doing away with the motorcycle policeman. He is a very necessary and useful adjunct on our roads, but he need not bother himself about speeding. We've some good friends in the traffic squad of our state and have always found them courteous and friendly. One officer, in particular, has become a sort of institution in the little village where we have our humble abode. He is of the old-time country "constabule" school, for our little village is so small that it doesn't boast a railroad connection, and to our way of thinking is even quainter and more delightful than Christopher Morley's beloved "Salamis," from which it is not far removed.

Our constable occupies his office on Sundays only. For the rest of the week we believe he is a farmer, but early Sunday mornings he takes up his stand at the crossroads, his uniform evidently not a Hart, Schaffner & Marx creation, for it is a little baggy at the knees and quite a little saggy in the front. But what are such trifles to the majesty of the law? All day long he blows his whistle, holding up a mighty palm to stop traffic and waving with a magnificent gesture to start it flowing again, in a manner truly worthy of an English bobby. Yes, we'd miss our "traffic cop" a lot in our village if he fell a victim to the onward march of progress.

But when all is said and done is there anything more impressive than an English bobby? The bobby is more than an officer in name; he is your friend, guide, and counsellor all in one. We love to watch Robert handle traffic. He does it so imperiously; he has only to raise that arm with its brassard, and traffic stops instantly. No loss of motion, no overexertion; merely a lifting of the arm and the restless myriads are still—truly a remarkable evidence of mob psychology, for a bobby doesn't even carry a pistol.

We were discussing this absolute control with a friend of ours who is a bit of a globe traveller. "Yes," said he, "it is remarkable. The moment the bobby raises his hand traffic stops instantly. Now in France it often happens that when the *agent de police* raises his hand for traffic to halt, it rolls merrily on; and in Italy, when the *carabiniere* puts out his hand, people rush up and shake it."

We cannot exactly vouch for the truth of this. Yet no one can deny that the French and the Italian have not the same reverence for the symbols of law and order that the British and ourselves have.

All in all, the British undoubtedly have the right to dub their police "the finest," even though we may claim such a title. But we are not far behind, and probably, except for a few individuals, quite up to the British standard. We had quite a striking example of this not long ago. For half an hour in the midst of a tremendous downpour of rain we'd been standing on a street corner trying to obtain a taxicab. In vain. The unoccupied ones that went by simply paid no attention to our frantic signals. Finally we appealed to the officer on duty. He immediately stepped into the street and blew his whistle for traffic to stop. Then he motioned to an empty taxicab to draw out of line, and as it drove up to us he opened the door for us to enter. As a final courtesy he stuck his head in the window and remarked, "And don't pay any more than the meter reads, sir. These birds'll gyp yuh every time they gets the chance."

Now, we ask you, could even a bobby have done more than that?

HORSE
(NOW EXTINCT)
Restored from contemporary
prints and spare parts.

The King Is Dead

THE horse, they'll tell you, is dead. He's outlived his usefulness. His day is done, and soon he'll be as extinct as the dinosaurus. They've been saying that for a great many years now—ever since the automobile was first adopted 'way back in the year 1900. They keep on saying it at intervals and will no doubt go right on saying it until Gabriel blows his trumpet and starts to wind up the business of this old world as a going concern.

Don't you believe it. The horse is far from dead, and just as long as there's a person who likes the feel of good leather under him, and just as long as there's someone who knows the thrill that comes only with the rush of the wind in your face as your horse clears the top bars and the hounds in full cry disappear around a corner after a streak of red—then just so long will the horse be monarch of all he surveys. That day,

praise be, seems far off. The revival of hunting
since the war has been enormous, and equine
interest has grown tremendously. All the great
hunts—the Radnor, the Myopia, the Meadow-
brook, the Onwentsia, the Rose Tree—are flour-
ishing like the proverbial green bay tree. And for
sheer spectacle what can compare on a frosty
autumn morning, with the trees a mass of red
and gold, to the sight of flying figures on magnificent mounts streaking across the barren fields
after a pack of hounds baying gloriously? And
what content can equal that which fills your soul
when, after a good run, you come home to a warm
breakfast before a cheery open fire? Here is the
very zest of life.

For that matter, what can compare with the
thrill of a group of horses coming down the home
stretch of a race track at full tilt, neck and neck,
with their jockeys urging them faster and faster
while the roar from the eager, excited crowd
grows more deafening? Who says the horse is
dead? If you think he is, go spend a week at Sara-
toga Springs, N. Y., in August, when the racing
season is on. Or drop down to Belmont Park near
New York on the opening day of a United Hunts
Meet. Or go out to the race track at Miami or
at Louisville, or arrange to visit Baltimore when

that classic of steeplechasing, the Grand National, is being run. We warrant you'll change your views.

And if there are further doubts as to the demise of His Majesty the Horse, how do you account for the horse shows that are held during the season almost every week in some city or other throughout the length and breadth of this great land of ours? At a horse show there is no interest save the horse. There is not the thrill of the chase, nor the excitement of the race either—just the love for good horseflesh that has been our heritage ever since the early days of the republic.

No, the horse will never disappear, nor will the interest in him. His place in our hearts is too secure for him to be replaced. The King is dead, long live the King!

And what of man's best friend, the dog? Is he gaining or losing in popularity? Is his day done, too? Anything but. For as long as there is a two-footed human being left on this planet you'll find him accompanied by his faithful four-footed friend. The canine grows in popularity as the years go by and you'll find him everywhere that mankind dwells, from the humble mongrel in the African's kraal to the pampered pet in the most luxurious home on Fifth Avenue. For the dog, in his various breeds, is a strangely adaptable beast, and hardy too, but none the less one who responds to the sunshine of affection.

Fashions in dogs change only a little more slowly than do clothes. Not so long ago the lordly Newfoundland was the children's pet *par excellence*. Where is he now? Vanished, indeed. And the fat pug with the curly tail, where is he? What has become of the scores of French poodles and the low-hung dachshund? They are the exception rather than the rule nowadays. Even the smooth-haired fox terrier and the King Charles spaniel have suffered eclipse. Instead of these old stand-bys we have with us in legion the police dog, the Sealyhams, the Bedlington terriers, the Dobermann pinschers, and the schnauzers—the latter unheard of to any extent in this country several years ago.

People seem to want looks in a dog as much as other qualities, and that is where pug and poodle lost out. The newer breeds in many cases combine good looks with other virtues, and that explains why they are so much in demand. Yet, contradictorily, almost the ugliest dog in the world, the bulldog, holds his position well up the ladder of popularity as securely as ever.

The increase in the number of outdoor dog

shows in the country during the spring, summer, and fall has increased the popularity of the dog enormously. The annual show of the Westminster Kennel Club is the event of the year in dogdom. We wander about this show each year trying to make up our mind which dog we prefer above all others—but we like them all, or almost all. For sheer looks there could be nothing handsomer than a police dog. But a brindle Great Dane at attention is hard to beat. While a pair of Russian wolfhounds, the way Marguerite Kirmse once delineated them in one of her famous etchings, can scarcely be equalled on the score of looks. A good chow is a lordly and handsome aristocrat, and the collie certainly is well up on the list when it comes to looks and also when it comes to affection and loyalty. A black collie with a white ruff is a regal-looking object, and the new strain of merles is perhaps the handsomest type of collie that there is.

When it comes to character one's heart is torn between the lovely, almost humanly sensitive Boston terrier and the pert, friendly, independent Scotties. We've had both and are still undecided which we like the better and probably always will be. Then cairn terriers, or West Highland Whites, or Sealyhams are all very intelligent and great playmates to have about. We've formed a fondness for the wire-haired fox terriers and the Airedales, while in some senses an Irish terrier is the most satisfactory dog of all. We think we could be happy with almost any dog, even a Kerry Blue.

As for the toys—the Pekes, the Poms, the griffons, the schipperkes, *et al.*—we leave them to the ladies. No doubt they have their good points, for one sees them on every hand, and they fill a useful rôle in a city apartment where no doubt an Irish wolfhound might be a little out of place.

Never, since we can remember, have we been without a dog, and we hope the day will never come when we'll have to be without one. For sheer companionship, devotion, and loyalty there is no creature on God's earth, to our way of thinking, that can compare with the faithful fireside friend, the dog.

"wh-wha-what's that building!"

"Oh, that's the new home of the cloak and suit trade, inspired by the business."

Sky-Lines

WAS it Maxfield Parrish or D. W. Griffith, we wonder, who first taught us to appreciate sky-lines? The former, you recall, loves to paint trees and figures against a background of the loveliest cerulean blue imaginable, while the latter was the first to see the possibilities for the movies of a group of galloping horsemen riding furiously along a ridge, or a string of camels outlined against the yellow sky of a desert sunset. You will recall in particular the dramatic charge of the clansmen in flowing robes in *The Birth of a Nation*.

But, after all, sky-lines were appreciated æons before these two geniuses flashed across the horizon. Probably the architect had a great deal to do with it. Certainly he has to-day. Who can gaze upon the spires of Oxford, or view the Sacré Cœur topping the heights of Montmartre in Paris without experiencing a real thrill at their beauty?

Or who can fail to enjoy the glimpse of rare beauty
—even though it be momentary—of the towers
of Princeton University, from a Pennsylvania
Railroad train as it dashes along on the main line
between New York and Philadelphia? It is the
one high spot of beauty on an otherwise tedious
and for the most part unlovely journey—a journey only to be taken through necessity.

Undoubtedly, however, the sky-line that
evokes the most comment is the sky-line of lower
Manhattan, with its fretwork of lofty towers and
buildings. Beautiful at all times, with a plume of
white smoke curling lazily from the pyramid top
of the Bankers' Trust Building, it takes on a fairy-
like quality with the coming of evening and the
lighting up of the myriad offices. There is nothing
quite to equal this anywhere.

For this great spectacle we are indebted to the
architects. On the woof of their imagination they
spun the web of concrete and steel that was to
give the world a new and beautiful expression
of art equal to the cathedrals and châteaux of
Europe and the temples and tombs of Egypt.

We do not know who it was who devised the
so-called zoning law, restricting the height of
buildings in certain sections of our great cities,
but to whoever it was the world in general and

America in particular owes a great debt. It has changed the sky-line of upper New York from a series of square boxes and towers into new, and for the most part beautiful and interesting, shapes. Buildings after reaching certain heights are built back so that the effect is not dissimilar from what we always imagined the famous Hanging Gardens of Babylon must have been. And the architects have eagerly grasped the opportunity that presented itself under this new style. They dared, and in daring have accomplished marvels.

The next time you are in New York look at the character and the individuality of some of the newer buildings. The Singer Tower and the Woolworth Building struck a new note, perhaps, but it was Harvey Corbett, who, if we remember correctly, really first achieved a new and happy effect in the Bush Terminal Building near Forty-second Street, designing a graceful skyscraper that had all the quality and feeling of the true Gothic. Then along came Raymond Hood with a design even more daring and novel for the building of the American Radiator Company. Here was a chance to do something different. His artist's eye visaged the nature of his client's business, which after all centred around heat—and

heat meant coal and flame. So he set to work
and designed a building to be finished in black
—like a pile of coal—and for the flames he topped
the building with little pinnacles and towers.
Finally, as a finishing touch, he gilded these pinnacles to represent flames.

The result was that he achieved certainly the
most talked about and—to our way of thinking
—a very beautiful and very striking building.
We have heard people condemn it up and down.
Others praise it to the skies. There seems to be
no middle ground; you either like it or you do
not. Personally we like it immensely, and we take
off our hat to the architect not only for his daring
spirit in casting aside the usual mould of convention but for the successful outcome of his
daring.

Gaze upon the Radiator Building particularly
at night, when the pinnacles are lit up by shafts
of light cleverly concealed below, and we wager
that you'll agree with us.

A building that intrigued us greatly recently
was the Ritz Tower in New York. Some forty-
two stories high, we watched it cast aside its swad-
dling clothes and grow tier upon tier. As it raised
its slim height like an arrow pointing into the
sky, it became a thing of beauty, even in its skele-

ton days when it was only a mass of iron girders pierced by the blue of heaven. Then they gradually framed it in—still a slim, graceful spear—until finally all was finished save the top, which was hidden by a maze of scaffolding. "Here," we said, waxing enthusiastic to our architect friends, "is another masterpiece." But some of them we must admit did not reflect our enthusiasm. "It lacks design," said one. "It is simply a series of boxes put one atop the other and set back at certain intervals from the street," said still another. But we held our ground. To our lay mind it was beautiful, and the architect had created a lovely graceful tower further to adorn an already handsome city.

But alas, our enthusiasm received somewhat of a setback. One fine day, chancing to stroll down Park Avenue in the cool of the evening, we cast our eyes aloft as was our wont to feast our eyes upon our concrete protegé. The last vistage of scaffolding had been removed, and lo! there, crowning the lovely shaft, was a sort of miniature Washington monument, hideous in its banality, with four miniature obelisks at each corner—the sort of thing one might expect on a lodge of the Mystic Shriners, but to crown a thing of beauty with a cap of that sort seemed almost a sacrilege.

So it is that for the time being our enthusiasm for sky-lines is somewhat abated. We shall confine our attention in future to pastoral sky-lines —a man ploughing along the top of a hill or possibly that other source of beauty, a big ship steaming along the horizon, or little schooners sailing demurely into the sunset.

For after all, Nature—the master architect—can never add a jarring note to the beauty and the perfection of her sky-lines.

"Thash shtoo many clocksh t' build sh' closhe t' one 'nother 'caushe look at 'em— all keepin' jush' the shame time! Sha washte of good clocksh!!"

High Lights on Life's Canvas

WE LIKE to think of life as a gigantic canvas on which are depicted all the events that go to make up our earthly existence. Fate is the artist who wields the brush, which is ourself, and the colours are our emotions and reactions. Some canvases are entirely sombre; others glow with spirited luminosity. The majority, however, have some of both sombre and gay. On such a gigantic canvas as life there must necessarily be occasional high lights just as there must be some sombre pigments. But it is the high lights we remember most frequently—those spots of colour caused by some deep-seated emotion that stand out in sharp etched relief against the monotonous tones of life's background.

The high lights in our existence, it seems, have to do with war, or rather with the end of war. Which is perhaps not unnatural, for war must stir the emotions as nothing else, particularly when one is an active participant or close enough to feel the horror and suffering that war entails.

This probably accounts for the reactions that were ours, in common with millions of others, when the Great War finally ended.

The first high light—perhaps the most joyous of all—was Armistice Day in Paris, for we were fortunate enough to be there when the great day arrived. Early in the morning of November 11th the air was surcharged as if with electricity. Paris was astir early. People went about their business quietly and unostentatiously. As the fateful hour of eleven approached, shops and offices began putting up their shutters. Little knots of people gathered in the streets talking quietly together. As the minute hand moved steadily toward the hour the streets became quieter, the taxicabs even ceased their clamour. Suddenly the hour struck. A gun boomed. For a fraction of a second there was a tense soul-searing silence, then pandemonium! Every bell in every church rang out a furious peal, every whistle blew continuously, and above everything else rang the joyous shout, *"L'Armistice est signé."* At once a hundred parades started; from every doorway, from every house and every building people hurried forth joyously. Men, women, children, *grisettes, grandes dames,* and *midinettes* joined hands together and danced up and down the streets. No one was allowed to pass;

each must fall in line. Music of every sort was hastily improvised. Disabled veterans headed each parade, and flags blossomed forth miraculously. The statue of Strassbourg in the Place de la Concorde, veiled in mourning for forty years, was the focal point for the masses. Buried under garlands of flowers there was still room for a foothold for silver-tongued orators to scramble up on and deliver fiery speeches which for the most part couldn't be heard through the continual cheering that went on.

When night fell, who could describe the scene? Who can ever forget the sight of the Grandes Boulevards? Jammed to suffocation, progress was well-nigh impossible. Everyone was dancing or shouting, and everyone fell to kissing everyone else. A taxicab tried to force its way through. Fourteen soldiers boarded it. They hung out of the windows and they swarmed on the roof. Four weary and indignant tires gave four simultaneous pops and collapsed—cause for further cheers—but no one minded, not even the driver. Processions wound in and out of the cafés, so all the patrons betook themselves to the table tops. About midnight a famous opera singer appeared on the balcony of the opera house and sang "La Marseillaise." Somehow we found ourselves on the opera steps joining lustily in with "*Allons, enfants de la Patrie*" and, when that was finished? "God Save the King," followed by "The Star-Spangled Banner." We even recall roaring out the words of "Oh, Canada" with a group of friendly Canadian soldiers.

Too quickly the dawn broke. The last thing we recall as we wended our way homeward in the eerie light of dawn for a few moments of fitful sleep before the celebration started all over again was seeing a little group of men and women dancing wildly around in a fountain regardless of the jets of water playing over them and singing "Malbrouck s'en va-t-en Guerre" at the top of their voices. For sheer abandon Armistice Night in Paris can never be duplicated, we are sure.

The next high light followed a few days later, a more solemn but none the less stirring event. It was announced that the Cardinal of Paris would sing a *Te Deum* of rejoicing in Notre Dame Cathedral the following Sunday. Here was history in the making! We set out early for the venerable cathedral on the banks of the Seine. Even though we arrived three hours before the hour set for the ceremony, the great square in front of the Cathedral was already a seething mass of humanity. It seemed hopeless to try to get in, but a friendly *sergeant de ville* and our American uniform saved the day, and we found ourselves inside but behind an improvised barrier, through which, however, we obtained a good view of the altar. We were admiring the great vault of the Cathedral and the flags of all the Allies draped about when a sudden surge of the crowd behind us pushed us violently forward. The wooden barrier bulged, gave way with the strain, and collapsed utterly with a tremendous roar. We were carried on the crest of the human wave to within a hundred yards of the altar when order was restored. From our new point of vantage we could see and hear everything. Opposite us were the great ones—Marshals Foch, Joffre, Gallieni, Poincaré, and Clemenceau, and others too numerous to mention. The Cardinal, in his brilliant robes, conducted the mass. It was a colourful and impressive spectacle, but the great moment came when the organist played "La Marseillaise." How the great organ throbbed and almost sobbed as it thundered out the mighty tune. One felt one's self lifted by a tremendous spiritual exaltation. On every side people were sobbing and singing alternately, and all the while little chills of emotion kept coursing up and down our spine. Surely *here* was the greatest thrill we could ever experience!

But we were wrong—there was still a greater one in store for us. And that was a few days later, when we witnessed in Brussels the triumphal return from exile of the King of the Belgians to his beloved people. For two days we had followed the trail of the retreating Germans across a blackened and blighted land. Despair and desolation everywhere, and then we arrived in Brussels, the evening of the day before the King was to return. Here was Armistice Day in Paris repeated again but with just a little more seriousness and depth of feeling. The Belgians had been under the iron heel of the invader for four years and their rejoicing must necessarily be of a deeper nature. But it was none the less spontaneous. There were very few American troops in Brussels, and the majority of the population had never seen an American uniform, but they knew it to be that of an Ally, and that was enough. Their reception of us was positively embarrassing. Crowds followed at our heels in the street; once we entered a shop to make a purchase, and when we came out a crowd blocked the sidewalk. At our appearance a great cheer arose, hats were flung into the air, and we were hoisted onto strong shoulders. All this was very embarrassing, for thanks to physical disability we had played only the smallest rôle, not even a fighting one, in the conduct of the war; but it would never do to disappoint the enthusiastic Belgians. So we huzza'd as loud as anyone.

There was no sleep that night. We went from one café to another; we visited the lovely old Place de la Ville, looking too ethereal for words in the moonlight, and festooned with the pennants of the Allies. For the entire city was a mass of bunting and flags, even the famous Manniken being elaborately garlanded.

After an hour or two of fitful sleep we were up early next morning, for we didn't want to miss anything, and the King's entrance was scheduled for 10 A. M. We had very kindly been given seats in the official tribunal, but we decided we'd rather watch the procession from a more informal position. So we accepted an invitation to share a balcony on the main street with a kindly and hospitable Belgian family. And we were glad we did, for we felt then as if we really belonged in the picture. The streets were a black mass of people. Progress ceased altogether. The school children of Brussels, each with a miniature national flag, lined the curbs. How they cheered and

shouted! And how they sang "La Brabançonne!"
They must have sung it a million times if they
sang it once. How anxiously they looked up the
street to see if the procession were coming, and
how eagerly they cheered any passing soldier or
official! Even a little dog trotting amiably down
the street came in for such a share of thunderous
applause that it set him to barking lustily. Air-
planes wheeled and dipped overhead, and we, on
our balcony, chatted and laughed, almost hysteri-
cal from excitement.

Then a tidal wave of cheering rose from the
streets below. The King was coming! Instantly
everyone jumped to his feet and every hat came
off. A burst of martial music, and the head of the
procession—a division of the brave little Belgian
army—marched by as jauntily as if they'd only
fallen in for dress parade instead of having fought
for four grim long years.

Then, in an automobile, in a tricornered hat,
came Burgomaster Max, the idol of Brussels, who
had bravely defied the Germans and time and
again risked his life for his fellow citizens. Following him in the next automobile came Bel-
gium's hero-saint, the venerable Cardinal Mer-
cier. With his scarlet robes draped about him and
his snowy locks blowing in the wind, His Emi-

nence rode serenely along, the right hand raised in benediction as he blessed his beloved people who automatically dropped to their knees until he had passed.

And then—moment of moments—came the King! Mounted on a snow-white charger, clad in his field marshal's uniform of olive drab, with a steel helmet, his hand steadily at the salute, rode the great King Albert. On his right, on a prancing black steed, was the Queen, and on his left Prince George of Britain. Behind them rode the three royal children with the lovely little Princess Marie José in the centre. What thoughts flashed through our minds! It was as though some old fairy story had suddenly come to life, and we expected the King's steed momentarily to cast gold shoes!

Useless to describe it; only a Michael Angelo could paint it anywhere near adequately; but as long as we live we are certain that nothing can ever surpass the scene on that clear November day in Brussels when we stood on the balcony and watched the King come home.